the cyclops review 02
Contemporary Poetry and Prose

the cyclops review 02
Cyclops Press

chief editor Jon Paul Fiorentino
editors Geoff Lansdell, Sarah Steinberg

Cover and book design: Rayola Graphic Design
Typesetting: Clive Holden
Printed and bound in Canada

National Library of Canada Cataloguing in Publication

   The cyclops review 02 : contemporary poetry and prose / chief editor, Jon Paul Fiorentino ; editors, Geoff Lansdell, Sarah Steinberg.

ISBN 1-894177-13-4

   1. Canadian poetry (English)—21st century. 2. Canadian fiction (English)—21st century. I. Fiorentino, Jon Paul II. Lansdell, Geoff III. Steinberg, Sarah

PS8233.C93 2002   C810.8'006   C2002-904191-0
PR9194.4.C93 2002

Agented by Signature Editions

The publisher and author gratefully acknowledge the financial assistance of the Canada Council for the Arts and the Manitoba Arts Council.

Cyclops Press,
P.O. Box 2775, Winnipeg,
MB R3C 4B4 Canada
www.cyclopspress.com

Introduction

Welcome to the first annual edition of The Cyclops Review. Within these pages you will find a diverse selection of contemporary poetry and prose. Our editorial mandate was to select the very best work that we have come across here at Cyclops Press over the last year and to remain true to a vision of diverse aesthetics and poetics. The texts collected range from narrative-based, to lyrical, to political, to formal, to experimental. Some of our authors are emerging while others are publishing their work for the first time: Steve Smith, John K. Samson and Monique MacLeod to name a few. Other contributors are celebrated, established, award-winning poets, fiction writers and playwrights such as Catherine Hunter and Daniel David Moses. What links all of the texts within these pages is the outstanding quality and literary diversity marked by the unique voice of each author. This anthology captures the very best of the literary press experience.

While the writers of The Cyclops Review are exclusively Canadian this year, future editions will reach beyond Canadian borders and include a significant amount of contemporary poetry and prose from the United States and Overseas. The expansion of our literary horizons is already well underway.

This first edition of The Cyclops Review will be accompanied by an extremely innovative multimedia component: a multimedia website featuring audio art, music, spoken word and experimental film. Please visit www.cyclopspress.com to achieve the full Cyclops Review experience.

This project would not have been possible without my fellow editors, Sarah Steinberg and Geoff Lansdell. I wish to thank them for their patience, support, insight, and impeccable taste. I wish to thank all of the writers anthologized in The Cyclops Review; this book is a celebration of their excellent work. I would also like pay tribute to the publisher of Cyclops Press, Clive Holden, for his passion for literature, publishing, his artistic integrity and for his faith in his editor.

Jon Paul Fiorentino

September 2002

Contributors

CYCLOPS PRESS

EXPERIMENTAL

Adrienne Ho

The Most Spontaneous Thing

Walking toward Bank Street in winter,
cold showing in our breaths. You leapt

pressed my back down
against what would have been
a raised flowerbed in summer, your mouth
planting kisses.

The whole few seconds,
I was thinking:
what if someone's looking, what if
in my backpack I carried some blown glass ornament
you didn't know about?

Orchids

The miniature creamer I bought at Harbourfront
now holds two stems of orchids,
shrinking away from the glare of day.

I hate to see flowers die.
The worst - irises,
rolled up lips and veins
like some unpreserved organ
split from the body.

Lifeless, it shifts into something less
and eventually becomes nothing.
Dust, waiting.
How objects find other uses:
inkpot candleholder,
an empty matchbox - coffin
for a shriveled weed from a field in Toronto.

Receptacles of the unexpected.

Michelle Sterling

ohtokyo

Oh Tokyo,
how you have hurt me with your automated urinals,
compact meal trays,
video game cartridge intersections.
On rice fields you stole gridlines of the sky,
cut and pasted shadows of boxed windows.
And I see you in your cubicle,
face pressed up against the drywall.
Oh Tokyo,
please pass the ginseng,
I am growing old with you.

Oh Tokyo,
you have smeared concrete between my ears,
filled my lungs with baby's cough,
emptied my bowels for canned dog food.
Remember when you spun around,
and saw your face in yawning storefront windows?

Oh Tokyo,
I am beginning to long for your metallic touch.

Oh Tokyo,
it's a suicide drive out there.
Spread me on sex shacks and interactive televison.
Litter my words in sewers,
over digital freeways.
I have stretched my skin around you,
felt your seconds against mine.
Oh Tokyo,
please swallow me whole.

Kate Hall

Window I

Winter blows in through the shattered bathroom window.
A view clear through.   They will watch
from the alleyway as I try to wash myself clean
with scalding water and wind.
His smell slicked so deep in my hair
I can hardly wash it out.
But I have to remain.   I have to make some attempt
to clean up the mess,   even though it moves outward
    from this spot
over us   out of our hands
out with the steam until I am where the stars are
looking in like a God;   from that vantage point the whole
    thing
just one big mistake.
Outside the steam turns to sleet,
blows back in.

Window II: woman with yellow scarf

Rows of pristine white linen tablecloths
draped and set for dinner—
empty wine glasses shine,
cutlery, pure silver.

I peer through the window
at a woman laughing, a yellow scarf around her neck.
My reflection beside her in glass.
The shadows in the mouths are the same,
difference is in the teeth
my all-too-visible incisors.
I want to bite straight through, starting at the wrist,
swallow whole chunks of her,
tear her apart, break her down,
and take her in at the same time,
her perfect scarf falling into my hands,
and for a moment forgetting I hated her at all,
loving her in fact.

Monique MacCleod

Public Spectacles

Despair

The sun's shuttered fall through
a switchblade intersection.
Light decapitates just below
the hook of her open mouth.
A toque puckers, dead,
into her bare hand.
This is one way to hack at angular grief,
that taut anchor.
Sun floods her mouth.
I walk on.

Epilepsy

The oil stain's dark sprawl across
sweating texaco asphalt.
Midday casts it as a paralyzed shadow
under his body electric like tossed fish.

Inches from the street his caught mouth
wilts in tethered exposure.
This is enough to spill hands empty,
the slackening fingers.
Nothing identifies his body.
Walk on.

Language

The deftness needed to haul words against
the nervous vacuum of synapse.
Blink, and mind leashes onto the stun
of empty pause, drags it out into the open.
You keep on blacking inside
your own poems.
This is what the open mouth is all about,
an aphasic linguist.
What else can be said.
Walk.

Catherine Hunter

Theft

And now, beyond the television,
beyond even the front window
of your little house, out on the grass at the edge
of the Seine River, in the vacant
lot across the street, a car is burning. This is a test,
but you don't know it yet. There it is.
A 1995 Thunderbird in flames.
No, it's not some emblem of your lost youth,
a sign of recklessness, abandon. It's simply
a stolen car that pulled up while you were not
paying attention. The blank surface of the river
and the sleeping, working-class roofs
begin to glow, begin to seem combustible.
You rise from the couch and wake your husband.

When the electrical system catches fire, the tail light blinks
and the horn sounds, as if someone trapped inside
is signaling for help. You dial 911 and then it all becomes a blur.
That's what you tell your friends afterwards,

it was all a blur—two o'clock in the morning,
your brain full of sleep and television.
But sometimes, later, you remember what you saw,
though you don't speak of it. Your husband
running across the street, naked, as if he could pull
that unseen person out, before the gas tank blew.
Of course, there was nobody in there. That's the point,
as you like to repeat: there was nobody
in the fucking car. The trouble is you can't forget
your husband's body in its skin against the flames.
How willing it was, to leave you for a stranger. And now,
when he touches you, you're cold. There's a mean stripe
of heat across his palm, where he tried to open the handle.
But it does not warm you. When he drinks
too much, when he swims too far from the beach,
when he rides his bicycle with no hands, his two arms
open to the wind, you can feel how cold you are.

Work in Progress

At first, all you can think of
is that moment when you were twelve
years old, your toes gripping the rough
edge of the ten-metre diving board,
wondering if you'd go over, and when,
and whether you'd survive. Then you remember
those hot diamonds in the chamber of mirrors
at the planetarium, that deep, deep, glittering
space in six directions, yourself suspended, falling.
You are going down again, and why? You're leaving
behind the slight drift of cumin and ginger
from the rooms below, the dull pulse in your thigh,
a distant radio. Outside, there might be a windchill
factor of fifteen hundred or a flood
or maybe another boy smashing a stolen car
into your fence, but you have already gone
too far to know these things or care what time it is.
In here, it's always the middle of the night.
It's not a dream, although it's crowded as a dream

with ladders, closets, open doors — that steep staircase
you're always descending, your dead
friends speaking a foreign language.
There are strangers down here, too.
Sometimes they ask for your help, as if
you could rescue them. Or they lead you on,
pretending to know the location of your keys,
your socks, that letter you think you wrote
but never mailed — where is it? Why do you enter
and enter again this space where the laws
of logic bend like sunlight clinging
to the curves of matter? You keep on
traveling deeper, though by now you know
full well there are no insights here.
There are only mismatched gloves, stopped
watches, overdue books. Then darkness,
an inflorescence of stars, a splintering.
It was a long time ago you realized
you're not looking for anything down here
any more. You are one of the lost
objects. No one is coming to find you.

The Headache

The skull sparks, impatient in the blindness
of the bedroom, and though the shades are drawn,
the left socket cracks open under the closed eye,
drinks light through the skin of the lid.
What is it telling you, this bright throb of blood
through the temple? You guess it's the same old
story of the end of things and you
don't want to listen. Listen. When you were twelve
you fell on the skating rink and witnessed above you
the forked, hoarfrosted branches of lightning
like a maze, and when you were nineteen
you stepped into the road too quickly and then
you were allowed to see the long tunnel of light,
studded with snow and shards of headlight glass,
and when you were twenty-six you split in two
and they drew out of your body the radiant
living soul you call your daughter. And now
they are showing you again the white flame,
saying, *be prepared*. The flame belongs to you

and nothing is so lonely as possession.
Tomorrow, you think, and then you can't think,
brain a glimpse of scissor blades
and roman candles. Your daughter enters,
lays a cool cloth on your forehead, where it steams,
disintegrates into a sheet of ash.
You think you hear her voice, but you can't see
through the glare and when she vanishes
into the hot corona, then you know
there are no preparations. But you won't remember this.
The headache won't last. Not this time. Not yet.
Tomorrow you'll rise from the bed and bathe and dress
and walk into the winter streets. You'll count your coins
and buy a loaf of bread, a paper.
You'll sit on a park bench, reading. See?
The snow flakes and the sunshine whirl about your head,
cover your dark hair with a cool white veil.
All morning, all around you, the pale and temporary
darkness that's your life
is closing in.

Peaches

Nostalgia is the colour of plums,
it's a Greyhound bus climbing the highway
into Golden, British Columbia,
after it's passed through the orchards.
It sets its passengers loose. One by one
they roll across the parking lot,
buoyant, expectant. In their minds,
the ripe peaches are still falling
slowly from the sky. A sixteen-year-old
girl imagines her own body in the soiled uniform
of the waitress, her own fingers, wearing
bandaids, curved around the handle
of the coffee pot. In the mountains,
she saw waterfalls the colour of winter,
and a cougar. She could stay here,
she thinks. She could belong to Golden
and the cougar and the coffee shop.
She walks outside, carrying the cup
of coffee and heavy cream, hot in her hands.

The cold smell of snow descends from the mountains.
She crosses the parking lot, crosses the highway.
She crosses a clearing and enters the pine woods.
When the bus leaves, there is always
someone looking back, face pressed
against the window, because if you're close
enough to the glass you won't be blinded
by reflection. The bus moves on
through the high clean air, the plum-
coloured wind, with its cargo of dreamers
and their dreams, those orange globes
floating to earth, packed with sweet juice,
glistening with dew, like a postcard
of Golden, British Columbia, only
real. I know it is real,
because I lost it.

Rob Budde

Excerpt from the novel *The Dying Poem*

Dee knows Henry has killed himself. "Henry." Out of nowhere, for no reason, she mouths his name and knows he has killed himself. The knowledge is a sensation that rises—a new language, a single whispered utterance. Then more, quiet bursts of syllables, and these sounds form limbs, eyes, hunger. Dee's face, her countenance, her stiff social exterior, so practiced and precise, remains undisturbed. It is 12:21 pm and she knows he is dead. Henry. He is, Henry was. The knowledge is like a quiet contraction. A shift in chemicals. In that instant, the feeling fans up from her fingertips as if a cold glass of wine had just been handed to her. He is dead. The knowledge slides up her shoulder blades and settles around her neck. Henry is dead. She, outside herself, saying the words, "He is dead." An impossible knowledge coming to her without doubt. "Dead." The word resounds as she remembers his face as he stands at her door for the second time that first night fifteen years ago. He is holding fruit, of all things: a pear, two peaches, a kiwi and a mango. They squirm in his hands like puppies and begin to tumble down the steps. His eyes are on his hands, trying to control them. His hair is unkempt and he is wearing the same clothes he wore the day before, cords and a baggy gray sweater. He seems ancient standing there, a poet of the ages, decrepit and pure. Exuberant Athens, brooding Milan, weary London—any setting would have held him. He is a product of Western history standing there on a rainy night in suburban Toronto. He is a lyrical figure of speech, breathless and confident. It is not raining but it should be. Standing on the steps outside her door, he knows she is watching his face and will not help him with the fruit. Even though she stands barring the door with her arms crossed, he knows she will let him in and tell him what mango trees look like. His eyes will flash open as he tastes one as if for the first time. Then, he will tell her how desperately he wants to be a great man, how he wants people to remember his name, to read his writing. She is stunned by his blunt honesty but does not believe him. Instead she humours him, shushes him. Makes love to him. This last she does reluctantly, knowing it is a trap, knowing that men like him build monuments around their lovemaking, as if it is something significant. He does not know how to make love very well, she thinks afterward; he has a lot to learn about subtlety. She does not tell him this, but instead looks across the bed with pity, wondering if she should try to save him. He is dozing off. But this memory now teeters on the edge of absurdity. He is dead. That first night, even though in the past, sits precariously present on the edge of the idea of his death. That chasm, billowing into her imagination, swirls to fill all her concentration. And it is concentration—she cannot help but imagine death more vividly than she ever has before. Not just those late night swoops into vertigo, the thoughts of what nothingness feels like. Beyond that. Part of her consciousness has followed him. She is curious more than anything else. Dee's mind addresses knowledge as if it were an intruder, as if she has caught language in her back yard late at night, as if it stands between her and peace. The loss of Henry almost seems trivial in the face of the question. Yes, the question. She stops and looks directly into a light-bulb in the lamp beside her. She is not sure where she is for the moment. Her arm droops behind the chesterfield and she lets her drink drop delicately onto the carpet. She does not even bother to imagine the red fanning out into the weave of the white berber. The Goldheft Art Gallery reception is winding down, dwindling into clean-up. The cheese platters are nearly gone, glasses and smudged napkins cover the tables. The room smells like old wine on old lips. While all this is swirling in her mind she has managed to shut out the gallery crowd. It does not take much effort. She has suspended a conversation with a Winnipeg editor who is probably going to ask her to dinner. White salt stains spatter the bottoms of his pant legs. He published one of her short stories, a fairy tale that begins with a dream and ends in chaos (or what she thought at the time was chaos but since then she has seen the deception, always the deception). That was about three years ago and he has tried, in a cloying, pawing way, to keep in touch ever since. Henry has not come up in the conversation. She leaves the party graciously. No one notices her change in mood as she pulls on her long coat and waves goodbye from the foyer. They mistake her urgency for an elegant exit and blame it on the demands of a social debutante. They imagine the glamorous dinner party she is hurrying off to. But there may not even have been a change in mood. Dee puzzles over her reaction as she walks down the wet sidewalk to her sedan. If there was a change, it is from an absence, like from not eating enough. There is no shock. It is not surprising. It seems fitting. As she drives, the city is reduced to light and dark shades, angles and space. She imagines what it is like to die as she descends under the 14th Street overpass. As she re-emerges beneath the belligerent dark clouds, she begins frantically shrugging out of her coat. Like grappling with an attacker she twists and lunges forward and to the side. The car swerves near the curb. Finally, she tugs it free of her and shoves it out the window. It lands in the street like a body tumbling to a stop. The streets are wet and empty and the dim outline of sun is jeering. She vows to never ever speak of Henry again. Instead, he made his death a poem. That is how I knew it was a suicide even before I found the note. Poems don't happen just like that. Life isn't poetic unless it's in a poem first. Poems are created, man-made. They are planned carefully, premeditated down to the last detail, crafted in order to be read. When he died, he had three books with him, as if to fill an afternoon of reading, but I know he had already read them. They were for show. Three books he brought into the deserted Metropolitan Library. It must have been for show. I can see him now. He is sitting cross-legged on the bare hardwood floor, his hands resting palm up on his thighs. Do we all believe we are prophets? The northwest wing of the Met used to be literature and philosophy but now is empty. Emptier than empty, because the ghosts of books and voices can't even find purchase on the floor stripped of its red carpet. Not even the imprint of bookcases and traffic wear remain. The arched roof is of wood and careful stucco painted a soft cream colour. Motes of dust drift across the strong shaft of sunlight that is pressing on a patch of floor where he sits. The sun-lit portion of the floor is as long as he is tall and as wide as his shoulders. One book sits open in his lap, two others open on either side of him. He is looking into space, at nothing. In his mind is the composition of his death, the whole artful arrangement of his own demise. Everything I seek. The room is a painting by Caravaggio; a splash of light, a crescendo of stained glass and the rest is meaningful shadow, shade off shade, descending into deep black, the mass of humanity. Henry's face is apocryphal—saintly and orgasmic, yet struck with pathos. There is no turning back, this is the way it must be. Strike me down. His poem "To the One" begins Buggered by the passing minutes, I am Just beginning to rise, full-throated A singing lamp quietly nocturnal, Flickering the surface of solitude, Flickering the face of mortality, Sliding away toward more sightly things. I want to dwell only on the singularity of this thought. On the library floor, his legs cramping up, he is missing his cigarettes. He did not bring them. Neither a wallet nor his cigarettes were found on his mangled body. The crisp air hurts his lungs. He breathes slow and hears a low rumbling like the end of the world. Space, his existence, suddenly turns to stone. Such is the sacrifice for poetry. They recovered his ruined body almost 24 hours later. It was twisted and torn and only barely held together. When they uncovered him, his left arm was miraculously raised above his head into the tonnes of rubble. Stretched straight up, his hand seemed to be reaching to touch something. Or as if to catch something lost in that chaotic last moment. A book was lodged in his chest.

Kilby Smith-McGregor

Cheap

There was a man on the bus. He was wearing two pairs of glasses. One on top of the other. He was carrying bags. Bags from the dollar store. Double bagged birdseed. The bags are so cheap that through the bags you see the birdseed. He keeps a boy in his basement. He feeds him birdseed. He takes off both pairs of glasses to sleep. That's the only time.

There was a man on the bus. You've heard this one before. He had two suitcases and two small girl children. He sat back while the girls hugged the pole. Their clothes are so cheap that you can see the birdseed through their clothes. His brow is furrowed. Where is the connecting bus? He takes the girls from the city. He takes them on a greyhound bus. Another bus. I wanted to say. I ride buses all the time. Don't be scared. Your mother doesn't need you as much.

There was a man on the bus. He was tall as a ballplayer and he loved his mama. Even when he buried her. He had a parcel. It lay in the isle. He kicked it. Maybe by mistake. The ashes spilled on the bus. The ashes are so cheap that through the ashes you see the birdseed underneath the ashes.

Even if the bus was lost. Even if they were buried alive. They were so cheap. You could see right through them. Sometimes they want me to. And I want to say. I'm not strong. I ride buses all the time. Maybe by mistake. That's not the only time.

Corey Frost

Five Minutes with the Communist Manifesto

The Communist Manifesto: In the revolution, we will all be digitally remastered.

The Communist Manifesto walks slowly out of the water and up the beach. It is absolutely naked. Meanwhile, a spectre is haunting Europe. At the secret headquarters, the workingmen of the world unite. A car chase ensues. The bourgeoisie is trying to escape with the means of production, but the proletariat is following closely in a Lada. As the vehicles careen onto the sidewalk, racks of value-added goods are sent flying. Oranges bouncing everywhere. The fruit vendor stands in the street, waving his fist angrily at the rear window of the vanishing proletariat. The bourgeoisie escapes. But later, the Manifesto, disguised as an electrician, infiltrates the bourgeoisie's private party in an abandoned factory. The bourgeoisie turns out to be extremely difficult to kill, and in the struggle they both fall into a vat of molten steel, which will eventually be used to build a brand new superstructure.

Problems for Discussion: What is to be done?

The Communist Manifesto is a document outlining the fundamental tenets of Communism. And, a whole lot more! It is also the opposite. For example, if an assassination occurs on the other side of the world, and the alleged assassins emigrate to this country, then what is my own personal moral imperative? What is this other country? We don't know. We don't know whether it begins with a B or an M. It may begin with some other letter we have never even heard of. What kind of government do they have? Who was this assassinated prime minister? Was he an evil despot who loved his grandchildren? Or was he a revered leader who promoted peace and made the people aware of their own pitiful inadequacies? We don't know. The country is too far away, and there are too many countries, and too many letters of the alphabet to begin with. How can we know these things? What can we do? And I need it on my desk by, like, yesterday.

Art and the Manifesto: The manifesto is always pathetic.

What, according to the Communist Manifesto, is art? Art is anti-capital. If anti-capital comes into contact with capital, the whole system self-destructs. All art is quite useless, according to Oscar Wilde, not unlike a popsicle stick inscribed with an impossible philosophical query. In a world where capital is matter, then art doesn't matter. The bourgeois artist claims that art is merely the repository of all human knowledge. In fact, art is the suppository of all human knowledge. Art itself, in its unlimited glory, should become a form of art. The French have a word for art. Art should be exercised every day. Take art out for a walk in the park. Throw the frisbee around. If you love art, tie it to a bench and leave it there. Walk away from it, ignoring its pleas. If it escapes by chewing off its own leg and tracks you down, it's yours. If it attacks you, you may legally kill it in self-defense. That's love. That's art.

The Dadaist Manifesto of the Communist Manifesto: Feeling Removed

Sadly, today manifestoes are falling out of popularity. A manifesto is rambunctious, and perhaps a tad over-earnest. In art, they have largely been supplanted by autobiography, and by corporate mission statements. It is difficult for the surface and the not-surface to agree, but I assume in my work that the not-surface is actually only superficially removed from the surface. The sub-structure and the super-structure are the same. Whether it is removed above or below the surface is unnecessary. Q. How would one recognize the Communist Manifesto on the Metro? A. Really it's about feeling good. Feeling confident. Secure. You have to have a dream. In the beautiful park, in the evening light, a breeze is moving the children in the lake. A frond is waving in the breeze. Think peaceful, think fresh. GO FOR IT!

The Triumph of the Communist Manifesto
("The manifesto has become a historical document which we have no longer any right to alter.")

Dear Mr. and Mrs. Oscar and Gloria Adams of Swift Margin, Minnesota:

I hear that you have a very smart dog. I hear that he can take the squeezie nozzle of your garden hose in his mouth and that he can spray your two-year-old kid, who is playing in the plastic wading pool, in the face. He knows that he will be rewarded with a twinkie because this is a very funny thing to do. Clearly, your dog is very intelligent. I'm writing, in fact, because I have something to ask your dog. I want to know if he would mind being featured in a story I'm writing. The story is about the Communist Manifesto. It's a great story with powerful dialog and international appeal. The ending is a bit anticlimactic. But a dog as smart as yours, Mr. and Mrs. Adams, would really make all the difference.

Yours sincerely,

(K. Marx, F. Engels, 1872)

Steve Smith

Drywall

But then there is always the drywall,
great sheets of it, stretched out for mile upon mile,
one piece mated to the next on countless ceilings,
in countless houses,
enough drywall to circumnavigate the globe,
while dusty men look up,
spy rough permutations in its white surface
and think of work to be done
and opportunities missed
and loves faded in history,
like old plaster rotting under a leaky roof.

David McGimpsey

Reunion

What is my news? Well, since graduating,
I've raked it in and I've tossed it off,
I've plucked the green peach and sodded the pitch;
that is, aside from noticing the moon
shimmering on saw bladed ferns in redwood
groves, I have learned two valuable lessons:
always floss and nobody wants to see
your collection of shot glasses. Mercy.
I did not cry when Henry Blake died, though
I died every time Kinch deferred to LeBeau.
"That is so you!" I'm sure we'll hear that; "you
were locked up nine months for passing bad checks?
That is so you!" Of course, my High School band
never made the big time, never backed up
Thin Lizzy on their "Boys are Back!" bus tour;
Maybe our band name, *Wee Willie Nelson*,
doomed us; I regret insisting on it,
regret writing it in Magik Marker
on the ass of my best acid wash jeans.

I enrolled at Buford Business College
and just let the cocktails do the talking:
leaving the academy under clouds
of vodka slosh and ended up working
on the busy side of the phone: "But, sir,
your agreement says you should pay us now."
Today, I supervise a fleet of young
phone hawks in both technique and blabbergab.
Admiral, that is just so you. Romance
came around for me more frequently
than *Ernest* movies and, alas, was just
about as annoying. There was Andrea
(do you know if she'll be reunioning?)
who wrote poetry about fast horses
and father figures in undershirts;
it was a miracle she was with me,
always pressing for what she called "the truth"
as long as the truth never again involved
a story that ends "whacking-off with hazmat
mitts." Who knew she'd serialize novels
about the sexual awakenings
of Toronto: "she kissed his smooth tanned chest
and felt free." O my asthmatic princess,
wringing your hands in napkins, your purse full

of neatly printed, scheduled "coffee dates."
Then there was salty Kathleen, who thrived
on the confrontation, who grew with each
"piss off!" who sprawled on rank sofas
and drank Pepsi while sitting in the tub.
Thank God she won't be there! I can see her
coming through the gym doors like a tank
through the palace gates in Saigon, flying
high on her own mix of Jagermeister
and milk, screaming "where is that stupid fag?"
And, finally, Pamela, who I used
to love, but who now says she has to try
to work things out with her husband. I asked
and she just laughed, saying "I really love
reunions, except for the part about
murder being a crime." That is so her.
"It's been so long" they'll say before turning
to say "it feels like only yesterday."
My father thought that the best way to fight
heart disease was to simply ignore it,
my sister screaming about his yellow pills.
I'm not so sure his approach wasn't wise;
my mother sits patiently by herself,
makes her own tea, her own little cheese plate,

and still laughs when a TV ad begins
"do you have diarrhea?" Through the years,
while the economy boomed and bulldozed,
while computers made life much easier
for secretaries and Britney fans alike;
while doctors fought AIDS and cancer still,
while populations soared around the globe
and citizens pleaded to save marshland
and limit greenhouse gasses for the sake
of the dooming tear in the o-zone; while
geneticists promised the dawn of the clone
and the Hubble telescope took pictures
of galaxies that folded neatly into
other galaxies, I took time to perfect
the art of the bummed smoke, the hindered dream,
the delayed comeback zinger, the late lunch,
the jealous funk, the revenge fuck, hollow
vows, saggy jowls, long happy hours,
debit cards, loose fitting pants, nighttime soaps,
don't bring up the past, the hyena's laugh,
blaming it all on nice people like you.
That was me in your medicine cabinet.
That was me hanging up just as you picked
up the phone. What's the theme of the Reunion?

"Always and Forever: This is Us!" or
"May God save us from more remakes of
Planet of the Apes"? It'll just turn out
everybody's all dressed nice, showing off
how our spouses taught us not to say "nothink."
Spruced from long apprenticeships in the malls
and cubicles since we left sweet Hoodlum High,
we know how to deny the neighborhood.
Good guys all, we'll hear, all shy and quiet;
nerds and geeks who forgive the only school
in the state to be closed due to "benzene
poisoning." We'll transform poor to cute poor;
cartoon Brooklyn poor or high Rydell High poor.
Will there be awards? I'd like to see that.
Can I put my name up for most improved
sense of persecution? Naturally,
the award for most exactly where we
all thought they'd be, has to go to Charlie
G., who smashed his Chevette into a pole.
Would I see that guy, you know, the guy I once
punched in the stomach for five delinquent
dollars, get up, fight the piercing feedback
of the microphone, accept his lame prize
as nicest guy, and weep for "the best times

of our lives"? I'm sure Nicey's all set up:
probably doing lines of coke off whores' thighs
while the whores' tax attorneys look on.
I will be at the reunion. I will dance
to T'Pau and I will do impressions
of old teachers 'til they pry me off the bar.
But there will come a time when it gets dark:
the lights against the wall will hypnotize;
in frosted mirrors behind the schnapps
I will see couples dancing and realize,
for me, it's never that different than waiting
for a late flight out of Newark, despite
the sequined dress of yearned for Sasha May,
despite the welcoming handshakes, I opt
for the vampire who lives behind the wall,
he has leather chairs and a rifle range,
a pet tiger that he likes to call "Earl,"
a desk to carve in the words *It's over.*
Alone, I'll smell the factories again
and retrace the steps to the shops of my youth,
where they sold candy made out of petroleum
and just one brand of soft, gleaming white bread;
I'll see shiny elbows on my sport coat
and, just like that, all attendees will seem

like fat rich kids on ponies. They never ask
if the pony's back is sore, they only
say "I wanna lollipop!" Wouldn't it
be great if the nicest girl, and I mean
the most legendary Jesus-Loves-Me queen
showed up all divorced and brandy-weary?
And, if, we excused ourselves to some long lost,
stoner's enclosure just made for bra strap
fiddling, and we'd satirize everything,
including Sasha May, including my
own dreams of a one-off and looking in
her green eyes to say "we better get back,"
as the band returns to play *Footloose*.
"I thought that was more of an encore"
I'd say and, sensing a despair we shared,
she'd take my hand and gently remind:
"Koo Koo, the nice thing about crawling
into the woodwork is staying there."

Robert Allen

Excerpt from *The Journals of Irony Jack*

(II)

Wilmington, Delaware, 1969   *October 21*

I left the note for Martha on the fridge where she'd be sure to see it, up high in the stratosphere where she likes to soak up the tears of clouds. Martha was a social worker, and very tall, and so far had our love sunk that she now stooped to do her social work on me.

The note said, 'the only emperor is the emperor of Jim Beam', which is a joke between us, and the only levity I could think of to stick into the gloom. I thought of telling her where I was going, but odds are she'd have it figured out before long, so I left it at that. I also left one of my last twenties, after filling the tank of a Jeep in the Motor Pool and buying a loaf of bread and some cold cuts for the drive, along with a quart of whiskey and a quart of ginger ale. I told the Motor Pool Sergeant I had to go to Camp Lejeune to check out some problem with their mainframe. The sergeant was wedging his overfull belly behind the desk, and nodded glassily when I told him I was going. Always go AWOL after lunch.

As I fired up the engine of the Jeep in our drive and headed towards the big wrought-iron gates at the highway, autumn brightness shifting past, sky-blue, green as late summer, military post white all a-dazzle in the sun, I was brought back with unbearable sharpness to the summer Martha and I had met in a dance hall in Asbury Park, how we'd danced under a painted moon, my head coming up to, and resting on, her cashmere-clad breast. One of my problems is that, with my height and the slight hunch in my back, I seem to attract the mothering type; and unfortunately, am attracted back. I had been a bit of a bastard with Martha, but figured I had taught her something: not again, or not easily, would she fall for someone whose only social capital was the ability to spin a good tale. Martha came from a wealthy, and sheltered family, who were as careful with words as with cash. I strung not many, and not too scintillating, words together, and we were soon making out in the back of her Rambler station wagon, with a scary abandon I had learned to expect from well-brought up women. Sex, like all of it, was good for a while, then less good, then something that was subject to cold-war type negotiations.

I had not done Martha any specific wrong, but felt half ashamed anyway, as if being more worldly than her meant being more calculating. My life, as you will see, had been nothing like hers, and it was this that impelled me to go over the hill in a stolen Jeep.

There were a couple of things...The Camp Police had been called in twice, once when I was outside our bedroom window drunk and howling like a dog. Drink is not always kind to me. I was under arrest for singing Joe Hill or some other revolutionary song to Major Benteen and some visiting brass from the Nicaraguan army at the time, but I was so indispensable in the computer room that Benteen never actually had me put in the guard-house, or even under guard. Same thing after the howling episode, though Martha almost killed me that time with a rose-patterned tea kettle. I wasn't so lucky after a bar brawl across the river in Trenton, when I knifed a sailor in the stomach for making comments about my sloping shoulder. It was only a penknife. The CO had me removed from active duty and put under house arrest for a week—not such a good idea as it turned out. Going crazy in the house with Martha, I inflicted a bloody cut on her forehead with a glass, full of water, I swear, and after she first threw it at me. All I remember about that is waking up in the blue hours of morning, crying in her arms like a baby, both of us sorry as sin. I always know when I'm going down fast, even during those short times I'm an angel.

My mother was a circus dwarf.

Did I mention that?

It's her who taught me to deal philosophically with the way I look, though not to drink myself to sleep when the philosophy doesn't work. It was easy enough for my mother to say. At barely three feet and proportioned per-fectly, she was cuter than a polished apple, and so immaculately to scale you'd never think of her as short. I was fond of her, I guess, but for years hadn't been able to bring myself to go and see her, or even write. Hardly a day would pass when I didn't think of her some, even if her picture was just tipping out of the deepest part of my mind when I awoke in the morning. Often, brooding on my own self while going about some routine task, I would hear her small recriminations in the soft drone of the mainframe.

•

On my way to the mess hall, October 20th, the day before I lit out, I'd stopped by the mailroom to see if anything had come for me. Sorting through a week's junk mail usually set me on edge for the rest of the day, but to be truthful I was feeling good. I was keeping it all safely bottled up – the sorrow, the moody regrets for better times and places, my growing fear that Martha was keeping something from me because she thought I was in too delicate a state of mind to take it ... that she was planning to say it was all over, in short. It's odd how repression of the truth can sometimes give you a giddy sense of happiness. As soon as I got half through the multi-hued and glossy circulars and saw the smeared, dog-eared postcard, I saw with a sudden clarity that the rest of the day would be spent in a whirl of fear and heartsickness.

Hearing from my mother has always shaken me up, and this time was no exception. Even when I think about it now, nearly forty years later, I can get no pleasure from the glorious pictures of that autumn afternoon, how late October light slid down the dirty sides of old Wilmington, giving her a lazy beauty, doubly pictured in the calm, oily river. Nearly all the way to Philly lay a golden red carpet of oak and maple, while the air — a sooty, sullied mixture of ocean and industry—hung rich and fragrant above the city. I close my eyes now and think of all that, the way it played with all five senses, clear outside of time. It hangs in memory for a second or two, until mother's written words speak over it, bringing me sharply back: standing by my mail box, squinting at those ill-formed letters smudged over the card —it was an arial view of Lake Bras D'Or, Cape Breton, blue jewel set in green—that I held in a shaking hand. The mail clerk must have thought I was having some kind of fit. She leaned over condescendingly with a kleenex, which I slapped away, wheezing angrily because of my asthsma.

My son, mother wrote, come too see me at Wash. co. Fare. octobre 22, 23, 24. IMPORTANT news!!

While this message tumbled about in my thoughts, Lieutenant Fair-weather came in. Turns out he'd seen the stamp on mama's postcard where usually nothing but fourth class postal permits appeared, and wanted to know who it was from. I was starting to make up some likely story when he snatched the card out of my hand and began to read it.

I had to jump up twice before I got it back, and fled into the can, where I sat in a locked cubicle with my feet up, reading it over and over. That big blond fucker came in and called out something from just inside the door, then went back out, while the door closed with a slow hiss. I heard him and the clerk laughing in the mail room. Perched on the toilet, knees up to my chin, I stared hard at my mother's painstaking little letters, as if some inkling of the important news she had for me might leak out of them. I did a lot of cryptography around then, and so I looked at her sentences sideways and upside-down, in case some obvious message lurked in the unread spaces. Maybe it was just impossible to read my mother, but there was just nothing there. The words were simple, barely legible, either rained or teared on. The card was postmarked Narragansett, RI, three days earlier. I flipped it over to Lake Bras D'Or again, in case the key lay there. The shot was taken from such a high promontory, so far off, that there were no signs of human habitation, just a scribble of roads, as cryptic as mama's writing.

•

Mother, as I said, was a circus dwarf.

Her show generally opened the season in Halifax on Queen Victoria's birthday. Then it meandered slowly down the east coast—Old Orchard, Hampton Beach, Newburyport—all the way to the New Jersey coastal resorts, in its annual pursuit of absolute tatteredness. Most years, with bankruptcy balanced tantalizingly close, like a high wire artist with cold feet, a last few shows in Virginia were needed to put together a fund for wintering over, which they did on Lake Okeechobee in Florida, in the company of a hundred other showbiz outfits.

In another week or two, the show would have passed close enough to Wilmington for me to drive over to their camp on an afternoon off, and not have to desert in order to answer my mother's summons. So why this siren call from Narragansett? And why was I risking the stockade to answer it?

It was late in the day, so I got a hotel room outside of Philadelphia. It smelled of industrial cleanser and, faintly, of cigar smoke. I watched a TV show in which a series of chained defendants took a lot of lip from a peevish judge. The judge just looked lost in his robes, and his whole trial lost in America. I remember very little about the turbulent summer and autumn of 68, not because I did not have my own hopes, and dreams, and loyalties, but because my own inward life was an endless series of rooms full of cheap motel furniture, like the one I was in now. At eleven the TV went on the blink and I went to sleep. Or tried. I got up later that night and read Allen Ginsberg's Howl, which I'd thrown in my duffel along with the food and drink. The words stood blankly on the page, so I screwed the cap off the whiskey, had a couple of belts, smoked a Pall Mall, and this time succeeded in finding the trapdoor and falling headlong into the dark cellar of sleep.

Next morning, early, I got up, had a single cup of bad coffee from the diner across the road, and left. I felt surprisingly good. The weather had held, and morning sun warmed the chilly morning.

As I weaved in and out of heavy traffic on I-95, I tried hard to wipe everything from my mind and just experience being a winking mote of consciousness in a skein of light and sound made up of millions of other feeble sparks. I looked at the brick backsides of old industrial buildings, sooty-red and shambling, looked at the cold curlecues of smoke writing new stories on the bored air, looked at the gold-glinting domes of innumerable town halls and cathedrals the length of New Jersey, Connecticut and Rhode Island, which I entered with a far shimmer of ocean to my right, and an unlofty, dusty green wood of maritime trees and tangled burberry bushes. By then it was midafternoon. I started to consult the map again.

All day, I had driven for an hour or so at a time, then stopped at Highway cafes, longing for human company, however indifferent. I'd sit at the counter with a chocolate milkshake, framed as likely as not by a couple of massive truckdrivers working methodically through the buffet. I couldn't believe the number of fat men on our roads—big, raw-boned, belly-slung men with rich, gravy-brown eyes. At the last stop before I reached Rhode Island—just outside of Mystic Seaport—I skipped the shake and just had coffee and water. Then I ate a ham and whitebread sandwich from my bag, smoked a cigarette, butted it, heaved a sigh, and climbed back into the Jeep.

The lovely fall weather had by this time itself fallen, getting more in tune with the dolefulness I felt. Not just Martha was gone, my career in the army was gone too—strictly speaking, I know, I was a civilian employee of the base, but the boys had made me a kind of uniform out of cut-down fatigues and some gilt braid. Fact is I must have looked more like a concessionaire. Anyhow, it was all gone, and at the age of twenty-one I could not see past the night, which was rapidly approaching, though the clock said it was not much past mid-afternoon. Oily clouds were boiling in from behind, and in the newly sprung-up wind dirty yellow leaves fell all around. I thought of Martha reading the note, with a bit of a smirk on her face to hide the heartbreak, then tears that broke like a sudden squall of rain. And knowing how the pathetic fallacy seems to infuse the narrative thus far, as you can bet the rain itself came then, ineffectually kept from the windshield by old, ragged wipers, so that I felt drawn down into an epic inundation. I rolled the window down to get a bit of a fix on the roadside, since I couldn't see much ahead. A single seabird, perhaps just a common gull, lifted up alongside, carrying in its beak what looked like a fragment of frankfurter bun. I thought then of Martha, still stood by the fridge reading my note. Would she see the encryption holding the words, cold as they might seem? She was the first one I loved, and something of my love went into that note, though the words were framed as accusation and self-hatred. One of the things I had written was, "I don't know who I am, Martha, and I have got to find out. In any case, what could I—what could you and I—have been? I am no more a lover than I was a tightrope walker or a ringmaster, or a clownish dwarf. I am my mother's towering, ungainly son, by her impeccable tininess impossibly patronized...." I had once told Martha of a dream: I was a dark child born into an icy world, frail and witchly in an umbered and unheroic land, full of big dumb blonds. I don't remember what, if anything, she had to say to that, or if she had, how she said it. I was entirely self-absorbed, burning with shame.

Grimly I rode the waves towards Narragansett.

Daniel David Moses

Buzz

It's not just you. A housefly's up and buzzing too,
buzzing that ten watt bulb the way you do your sleep.

It's good for the fly, how the glass keeps it well out
of the bright and alive. It's not quite so fine for

you that the fly's little whine has strung you up, strung
you out in the night, wired with fatigue, not quite

asleep, bumping electron thoughts not nearly clear
enough to let you even turn the light bulb off

the switch just there at hand keeps so far out of reach.
Oh you're so low in wattage, you're almost a bulb

yourself, well out of the dark and awake, the dark
you no longer mistake for a place to rest. Glass

once was so easy to break but now nothing is.
Nobody even dreams of killing the power.

How to Make a Fish Sweat

Jigging overhead through the haze the metal of
stars, so far away, won't lure more than eyes from bed.

The rest of our bodies, spread out at the bottom
of the night, even up on the seventeenth floor,

dive after the ice in the depths of tall, empty
glasses, searching for an alcohol clear shiver.

We find instead a stir in the heavy water
we're made of, a hot flow of salt rising into

muscles, nostrils, the shining cheeks of our faces.
The current the fan on the sill supplies never

will dry up the one in our skins. Oh our tongues shine
silver with the taste, spooning the submarine night.

Geoff Lansdell

Parallax

It was just after noon when Pete left the Liminal Institute with a tweed coat slung over his shoulder and an inanimate look on his forty-something face. Craning his head like a calypso's pistil, he looked out at the single-lane street below, examining its symmetry: sidewalk; parked cars; northbound traffic; median; southbound traffic; parked cars; sidewalk. Flawless, he thought, not a thing out of place. Except Jerry. But that was nothing new.

Jerry, who Pete had met while both were working on Astronomy Doctorates at the University of Arizona, had been highly recruited by many institutions for his practical expertise, receiving offers throughout his college years. But after choosing Liminal and moving to Colorado he had coasted. Whether he lost his verve for the field or simply hit a wall and stopped growing, no one could say. In either case, his work suffered. His habits grew porous. And the effect of these repeated oversights showed up as glaring gaps in his conclusions. Assumptions were made where evidence was expected. But Dr. Simon Liminal, who had inherited the Institute from his father over a decade ago, and did everything from the hiring and firing to approving research proposals before they were sent out to the National Research Council, refused to believe he had hired a dud, despite a growing pile of evidence to the contrary. So Jerry stayed on, his wiry presence twining between projects like bindweed, bungling research, stifling progress, and chronically falling short of deadlines.

"Pete!" The call of Jerry's voice from behind. "Sorry I'm late."

Turning to see Jerry's wan smile, Pete was struck by the weathered look on the familiar face of his oldest colleague. It was a face full of neglect. Under his knotted beard, Jerry's cheeks were a sickly green; below his vein-stained eyes, two oval bulbs grew dark as soil. And dandruff. His shoulders looked as though aphids had made the most of the breeding ground above.

"Jerry, where have you been?" Pete asked, checking his watch, "it's quarter-after twelve already."

"Yeah. You know how Sedgwick can be when a new idea springs to mind."

"Well sure," Pete conceded as he began down the steps and onto the sidewalk, "but I've been biding my lunch time for the last fifteen minutes. Surely it can't be so important that he won't let you leave when you have someone waiting for you?" When Jerry didn't respond, Pete continued. "Anyway, what is Sedge working on these days?"

"Something to do with singularities," Jerry began. "He seems to think he's found an example of one on Earth. Of course he's being pretty hush-hush about the whole thing. All he'll tell me is that he's been observing the collapse of a star into a white dwarf for several years now. And a recent collapse brought it to the point of infinite gravity and density. If this much is true, he has a singularity. But that much on its own is nothing to write home about. The peculiar thing, which is what he's working on now, is that he's convinced his singularity is tangible and has a variable event horizon. He figures that if he can prove the second part, the first bit is a given. Sounds to me a bit of a crock, but for whatever reason, he's insisted on having me as his lone assistant."

"Well," Pete said, "try not to strangle this one."

"I don't know that that's good advice in this case. I've already misinterpreted some research he asked of me. And then I lost most of a program he'd spent the better part of a week working on. But instead of ragging on me the way he usually does, he kept quiet on both accounts and sat down at the computer to write. Without a word to me."

"Well, maybe he's gotten used to you."

But Pete knew there was more to it than Sedgwick adjusting to Jerry's shortcomings. Could be some sort of personal vendetta Sedgwick has single-handedly decided to wage to rid himself, as well as the Institute, of Jerry. But Pete also knew how Liminal felt about Jerry. "The boy'll turn it around," he would say, "just a mighty slump is all." How any scientist could treat incompetence in such apathetic hockey terms was beyond Pete, but he hoped Liminal was right. After all, Jerry was a brighter man than he'd shown to date, but how to turn it around? And why had he never lived up to his billing to begin with?

Fairly certain Jerry wouldn't be fired, nor turn it miraculously around, Pete changed the subject to gardening. Of late, when he wasn't at the Institute, Pete had been taking advantage of the year's early spring to begin his pruning and get a head start on recovering from the winter's heavy snowfall.

"Been keeping up with the yard work, Jer?" Pete asked.

"In April? No, I haven't. I don't expect you have either."

"Perfect season for pruning, Jer. Snow has ended, rains have washed enough of it away. And it's always better to prune before things begin to bloom."

"I don't know," Jerry said, "it's still too dismal to be pining my time away on a ladder."

"Well, I'll tell you right now," Pete began didactically, "if you wait until the first spring bloom to begin yard work, you're already too far behind. Gardening should never turn into a game of catch-up. If it does, and you only prune in the spring, you allow other things to fester. Your focus gets divided. And while you're wasting your time in the orchard in May and June, you let the wrong things grow. Morning glory. Thistles. And when these types spring up, you're fucked. They will plague the flowers you slave over; and I do mean plague."

At this, Jerry sort of smirked, unsure how to respond. For him, gardening was little more than a part-time pastime. Which could be why, year after year, his snapdragons were meek and frail; and his spices grew into garnishes and little else; and his orchids never made it to the dinner table. Considering these past failures, Jerry could feel that Pete was still waiting for a reply. Unwilling to face Pete's willing eyes, Jerry kept his head down as his cheeks flushed.

"Maybe," Jerry finally offered, the silence causing him greater discomfort than it did Pete, "maybe you're right. Only I'm not sure I mind dandelions brightening my lawn and wild flowers taking root wherever they spring up."

"Listen," Pete picked up, "all I know is that gardens are a full-time commitment. You leave the excess growth—the twigs, the rotting and broken branches—to the late spring and summer months, it leaves you no time to keep up with the other villains that weed their way into your garden. Some wild flowers may be fine, but what about morning glory? Tell me, what does it do but remind us how fragile the whole operation is? It strangles, steals food and light, and is near impossible to uproot. It turns order into bedlam. And if you don't stay on top of it, you perpetuate your problems. Take this street for instance. It's perfect. You put competence behind the wheel, weed out those who drive too fast, too slow, or lose control, and you can maintain the order. Otherwise things get tangled and nothing is safe. And then it doesn't matter how diligent you are. It's already too late catch up with whatever has been left to its own devices while your back was turned."

"I see what you're driving at Pete"' Jerry posited, "but this street has always looked like a graveyard to me. People pass through and that's all they do. It's hardly interesting."

"Right, people pass through. That's the point. There shouldn't be any interest. It's functional and that's all. An in-between, a way to get from point A to point B."

When Pete finished, he looked over at Jerry, whose head was buried and following the approach of a dried maple leaf. As they continued, the indolent leaf rushed at Jerry and clung to his gaunt stomach. And it stuck. Jerry smiled at the leaf's simplicity, but Pete, following this foolishness, was not amused. He said nothing, however, and closed his eyes, sadly shaking his head. Then he closed his left hand and swung his fist violently across his body, crumbling the leaf against Jerry's unsuspecting stomach and forcing the air from his softly wheezing lungs. When Pete let his hand fall back to his side, Jerry doubled over and desperately struggled for air. But after an initial gasp, inhaling more beard than air, Jerry dropped like a chopped dandelion.

"Listen, Jerry," Pete resumed in a calm voice, Jerry lying at his feet, "I think it's high time you got your mind off the cement cracks and whatever else you focus on. I speak to you and you've not a fucking clue what I'm driving at. I'm not only talking about gardening. Listen, there's no doubt you're clever and know your field. And I'm sure everyone at the Institute would agree. But they would also say they'd rather not have you as their research assistant. And there's no question you are difficult to work with."

Looking down, Pete noticed his friend struggling on the ground and extended an arm to pull him to his shaky feet. For a moment, the two men stood staring in silence, Pete looking typically placid, Jerry still gasping for air as the colour drained from his cheeks.

"Jesus, Jerry," Pete said, changing his tone and wrapping a congenial arm around his friend's shoulder, "we better get some food in you. You're not looking well."

Jerry didn't respond to this bit of insolence, but allowed his shoulder to be guided in the direction of the diner, which was now less than a block away. Too weak to react, Jerry also knew that Pete was right. At the Institute, Jerry was still given the same functions doctoral students started out with. And three years had gone by. Three years in which Pete had gone from research assistant to the top of his field. He was taking research projects to the National Research Council, receiving grants and directing his projects as they took off. Jerry, on the other hand, had grown accustomed to being a thorn in the side of his colleagues' progress. And for three years Dr. Liminal perpetuated the problems because his pride wouldn't allow him to ditch Jerry. This sad conclusion was nothing novel for Jerry, but having Pete, who had admired Jerry's practical ability, point it out was devastating.

With the garish green neon of the All Together Diner finally flashing into focus, Jerry and Pete were silent, the thought of food having neutralized their moods. As they stepped in to the familiar greasy spoon, Gloria, their usual waitress, applied her show smile to greet them, which appeared bright as a tulip, but was, in point of fact, as perishable as the wilted flowers on each table.

"The usual table boys?" she asked, menus already in hand.

"Fine," Pete answered.

"Coffee to start you off?" Gloria offered as Pete and Jerry slid into their seats.

"Please," Jerry answered. After handing out the menus, Gloria turned towards the kitchen, her smile falling from her face the moment she turned her back on Pete and Jerry.

Much of lunch went off without a glitch. It was the type of banal chitchat one would expect from two men, one hoping to avoid accusing, the other not wanting to be accused. But with the food came silence. And with silence came Jerry's self-consciousness. As he ruminated on the Sedgwick business, unsure whether he wanted an answer to the question he wanted to ask, Jerry raised his head, waiting for Pete to lift his from his soup.

"What is it?" Pete asked impatiently.

"Well, it's uh," Jerry stammered, "it's just that I was thinking and – do you know why Sedge has me working for him? I mean, we've never gotten along. Why all of a sudden? Why does he want me?"

"You want to know?" Pete asked.

Jerry nodded.

"What I think?"

Jerry nodded again.

"OK, here it is."

Pete paused to collect his thoughts.

"From what I can tell," he began cautiously, "you stifle Sedgwick. More than anyone else, his projects have suffered from your presence. So it sounds to me as though you are some sort of personal project he's working on. To get you fired or to figure you out, I don't know. As far as this 'singularity on Earth' business, it's a pretty thin veil. You are the singularity."

Pete stood up and dropped a ten on the table.

"Listen Jerry, all I can say is surprise him. I don't know what's gone on with you over these years, but surprise him. Even if I'm right, there's still not much point in backing out. You know Liminal won't do anything hasty, so you may as well prove you aren't this entity that is only capable of choking the life out of everyone around you." Pete paused for a moment, and continued when Jerry didn't make a motion to respond. "Look Jer, I'm sorry to tell you this, but when you look as defeated as you do, I know you can't be enjoying work. I just want to see you turn it around."

As Pete finished his glass of water, the two men were silent with the rest of the restaurant. Most of the men had returned to work and the only sound was the rumble of the fan overhead.

"Jer, look, I've really got to get back. Do you mind? We'll talk later."

Jerry shook his head.

After paying the bill, Pete walked into the street and pulled the bagged thistle out of his pocket. After considering it a minute, he stuffed the thistle into a garbage bin. Jerry, still inside, watched the street corner as Pete headed back to work. Jerry's thoughts wandered to his children. He wondered whether any of them would grow up to be different in kind than their father. Whether they would have any more drive. But just as images of his children played in his mind, a driver screamed through a red light and t-boned a random car. Jerry looked to see if Pete was still in sight, but he was nowhere to be seen.

Jack Illingworth

Pan and the Geese

"But I have satisfied myself, by long observation, that nothing but the gradual diminution of our forests can accomplish their decrease…"

—Audubon

Pan lay in the field, belly full
of beer-drunk, head sky-
clear, almost empty,
maybe thinking of Marlis.

Two Vs had passed that morning,
but he'd just winked at them, the day
early for a shot, idleness in the chill
air finer than an easy kill. Pan
smiled as the third wedge came,
wings quick and out of phase, honks
no chorus, just a breaking shout.

But Pan noticed, blinked, squinted:
there—the right tip of the V—eh? A small one,

a speck, surging ahead, almost thought-swift, soon to pass
the point! He leaps up, shoulders, and sights—squeezes off
a shot—and down it rushes, falling into the muck just past the fence.

In the likely furrow, a mess
of blood and slate-blue
feathers: a fat passenger pigeon, brown
sharp tongue just pricking
through its parted beak, feet curled,
wedge-tail smashed by the blast.
Not a goose, won't feed them
for days, but it's a night's treat
for Marlis.

Pan, lucky

About a year after Marlis left, Pan won at Lottario—
not too much, about five grand. He didn't tell
anyone, just sat on the money for a couple of months.
Then, in early October, he called up a taxidermist,
one that makes graphite fish for conservationists,
phonies, and braggarts. Pan paid the man one thousand
to design a two-foot long deepwater sculpin,
and had him make eight of the things, at fifteen
dollars an inch. They were beauties, fat spiny
tan, with pale bellies and dirtbrown stipples on
their heads and backs, mouths halted in mid-gulp,
spiky fins spread, spines pointed enough to pierce
a thimble. Their heads were broad, flat, stout, outsize
on these trophy bottom-minnows. The taxidermist
was sent a list of addresses, and bundled his work
off to Marlis, to the Premier's office (with a thank you
note), to the Reeve, to the local paper, to Rose, to Pan's
old high school, to the Customs office. He had been
told to keep the last one, as a tip. It's now on the

wall at Ryden's Border Store, with their sturgeon, their jackalope, and their beer-drinking bear.

Chandra Mayor

August Witch

Cup your hands around the word: August. Press your palms together and slip between the syllables, twist and work your fingers around the letters. Release the first long moan that rises like a supplication from an open throat, like sidewalks singing shimmering in the sun. Pry into the g, exhale and tumble through the thickening air, gathering and rolling into lightning fractured skies, gulping rain with pore and tongue and leaf. Caress the little vowel, its sweet brevity belatedly remembered. And then the sibilance, the heavy-lidded indolence of s, the bacchic homeless wasps stumbling from the nests, the split and sticky fruit and its electric trickling juices on your lips and chin and snaking down your hands. Snap your fingers sharp against the t while asters blaze and trees begin to flick the first orange leaves in crackling puddles at your feet.

Hold this in your mouth before you speak. Taste this word. It's as reverent as a carrot stretching swollen in the ground, full and firm as corn beneath the husk. It's as bitter as beer and trembles in delicious agony like sleep and apples and suspended breath.

Cup your hands around this humming buzzing word with scrabbling fingers, and abandon. Scatter the sounds like dandelion seeds, stubborn and ephemeral as blazing eyes, opened wide and rooted to this newly birthed and fierce, loamy body.

August cannot contain itself. Words and worlds split like pods of promises, over-ripe. I clawed and caught and hooked my fingers, cleaved and burst apart and found you, child of heat and storm, abundance, exultation: August witch.

Babel

My head is a hive, paper
thin, patched with spit and sweat and
scavenged scraps of sealing wax,
faded photographs of me and
me and others I've forgotten. Bees,
hornets, and wasps rustle in the catacombs,
stupefied and slatternly in their mumbled
grief, disbelieving the severance
of thread that once clutched
abdomen to thorax; the snag of shredded
wing; the dull and brittle carpet of shed
fur; the raw glimpse of skin; the sting
squandered.

It is always the end
of August here, the humid gasp:
always the stultifying cavity
that throbs between the seasons.

I press my fingers to my temples,
try to numb the whimpering and droning.
I did not cultivate these crippled insects.
I do not want these squatters. I do not cup
my hands and proffer promises of sanctuary,
haven. They built this hive, this monstrance
to themselves, without my hands. I do not
know which other life I thought I was creating,
nor how I did not notice the construction
of this legacy of obsolescence.

This is the place you find yourself,
then, the way a body wakens on a riverbank
after a beating: ribs and tissues splintered,
swollen, self-absorbed and fluent in the babble
of untenable, the brain and tongue still stuttering
in amnesia. I am the mute and renegade
neuron, the conscious chasm gaping
before remembering, naming, speaking: *wet shattered*
boots lips me blood where help
and here. I am the long, thick, pause
where the uninvited fall
in. I do not know how
they find me.

The labyrinth in my head is dank
and over-crowded, passageways maimed
and trepidatious. My tongue is twisted, viscous,
sometimes mistaken for honey. Sometimes
a bee with limbs intact and memories distilled
to crisp delusion will make the pilgrimage
to my mouth, declare herself a prophet,
demand a revolution: order me to speak,
to propagate, to spew her visions out like pollen.
I will not be Cassandra for these tiny, tattered
impotents. I coil my tongue and snap
them up like fly-tape, grind their insubstantial
bones into the ridges of my molars. Their message
is always the same, and does not fit inside my mouth:

*It is always June, always sharp, pristine, and barely
breathed on. The sun is a voluminous glutted
buttercup, air and eyes are nectar-sodden,
invincible, and all the grass is strewn with fat
white limbs like larva.*

When did I become the drone? I don't know
how I caught and clung to this collection,
this derangement, this disease. My hidden

legion wants me to continue their contagion
but I will file my teeth to blades, seal them up like battlements.

These are not my words, I
write. These are not my words.

Jason Camlot

Selections from *Botanicals*

Leaves

It will be helpful to consider every   leaf
as a separate portion
to be sung.

We do possess some facts:
The greenish-black ones are like a tree's turtles.
There is the fact of dew; and in the center
rib or spine are veins.

This said, much is still unknown.
The division of the breeze by the leaf petal
gives but a faint image of how the wind felt.
Also there is the mystery of "green leaf."

From a sentimental angle we can observe
how some people collect them as keepsakes,
like dried confessions, and how our love
of the leaf is shown in tracery.

Their physical properties are surprising:
Though airy in handfuls,
there is much weight within
a single leaf held by its stem.

They keep well in winter,
and sometimes like jagged mouths
they appear
frozen in the lake ice.

And then they suffocate in shallow pits,
are digested with wood,
and transformed
into charcoal and muck.

My botanical books speak
of exogenous stems
plunged into lead.
I don't in the least want to know what this means.

I prefer to understand them
as the ground's trembling scales,
the soil thus sung
in a choral shiver.

Stems

One never thinks
of the stalk.
For instance,
grape-stalks with no grapes:
the little feet
like an animal's feet
hooking without
fruit.
Every living
ripple or jag
grows wild
upon a stem.
The profile
of the letter
I
resembles
a human shoot
from very far
away.
And deep in the 586th page
we find the Yew
Tree etymology,

the roots reaching
back up inside
the trunk's core artery
like worms
searching for lost vowels,
their other hearts:
a e I o u.
Mapul, thorn, bech, hasel, Ew.
And don't you
ever wonder,
"If I were
a Tree...?"
Ugh.
Quite right.
The growth of sadness
is patient work:
a dead
sorrow ever
insoluble
in a living one,
a rosary with
but one berry
overly swung.
Using alike

our lips
and brains
we try to
understand
our words,
our trees,
our words for trees,
our trees of words.
The wonder of it!

And not just that.
Look,
here is a little
thing:
the tendril
curls.

Flowers

The flower's death is an offering,
like dust falling
into zones of fire.

In summer we come upon the gifts
of bracts and stalks and tori and calices and
corollas and discs and stamens and pistils.

Take that cluster of bog-heather bells.
Bunch them into a star.
They can only be drawn as they grow.

Take the dark contortion, the pale
wasting, the quiet closing of
the brown bells of the ling.

Take this foretaste of death-
flowers, their heavy wavering
like the gait of human bats.

Take this tiny red poppy,
all silk and flame, burning

in its own scarlet cup.

If you offer a small bouquet
of four, one pair is always
smaller than the other.

Take this humble host
of green syllables familiarly
Englished into nectar!

Take them from me gently,
and then cast the severed leaves
away.

Melissa A. Thompson

Nibble-Nibble, Gnaw-Gnaw

There is very little to fixate on in a dentist's office. No matter how swanky, and Doctor Benji *is top of the line*, the waiting room will always have the same watercolours of wheat fields, the same pipey-modern chairs, the same sterile air. Breath mints and enamel. No place to fix the gaze.

Out of everything, this is what is upsetting me the most. I can't pretend that I am anywhere else but here, blithering to a heap.

"Honey, believe me—I have contacts in this business."

She is rubbing the back of my hand frantically, my own mother giving me a Chinese burn. The mucus is running down my lip.

"He's a dentist to the stars for god's sake" she says, burrowing into her big horsey purse for Kleenex.

I hulk over to the left and finger at a 1995 issue of Chatelaine. *Unleash the Diva Within.*

Mom sits back, exasperated, the tissues blossoming out of her hand. I close my eyes and count the damage with my tongue. Three slices, from centre to the left. My mouth is filling with the coppery taste of my own bad blood. I'm practically a pygmy now with these triangle teeth. A pygmy with a mouthful of pennies.

"Gwyneth Paltrow" she whispers forcefully, not looking at me at all, but slicing into the air with a fistful of tissues.

"All caps."

I pour my head into my hands and my hands into my lap.

All caps.

There are all kinds of people doing fantastic things all of the time. It is exhausting. If I learned anything in school, it was this. When you are the type of girl who walks around with her body in a sort of feathery blur, the sharp, precise qualities of such people tend to become very attractive. It comes down to this.

I came to this conclusion in the alley behind Jojo's Arcade. Somewhere between the dog turds and the man-tooth, the flash-wrappers and the gravely gutter-run, I realised what was happening to me. And I decided that I quite liked it.

Hannah is the type of girl who could run you through like a rototiller if she wanted to. The kind of girl you like to have on your side. We worked together for two months before I knew. The bakery is a small place, with not much room for enemies. And I already had one.

There was something terribly fetid about Serge. His body took up a lot of space to begin with, and then there was this warm wet moving outwards, a hot yeasty mist that made my stomach wrench.

"Gret-chen" Serge would say, his breath wet on the back of my ear,

"Like th-is, like th-is."

He was always reaching a thick wrist into my things, speaking into the space between the back of my ear and my head. Whenever his arms, two meaty snakes, would slide out from under my armpits to knead at the dough, or push parsley into filo, I felt that I would vanish, vaporise backwards into each yeasty pore.

It got the point that I was feeling this way all the time, not only when his doughey crotch was in the crux of my back. I felt like an assembly of particles losing their magnetism, a collection of free floating entity. Eating became difficult. I felt that anything put into to me would fall straight to the floor in a half-masticated heap.

Hannah works the cash mostly. She's better with the numbers. I could never remember the prices properly; 2.89 for pumpernickel, 3.20 nine grain, 1.29 large baguette, .89 small. It's confusing, all those little bits, the pennies and everything. I couldn't keep track of them. But Hannah is good at it. She's quick. Quick and sleek and mean. When I would be in the back with Serge, rolling rum balls or mixing icing, she would stick her head in every once in a while to give him the finger. His back was always turned when she did it, but I know that she would do it anyway. She is that kind of girl.

We would take breaks together during the night shift. We would sit out back on the bread racks and she would have a smoke.

"He's a bad bastard," she said to me one time. Then she turned to see my reaction. I swallowed hard and felt my body puff out from under me like the feathers of a sliced pillow. She looked me up and down.

"My boyfriend could beat the fuck out of him", she said, not looking away,

"I mean, anytime you feel that you would like for that to happen."

Her elbows pressed forward, her body rolling slowly over her very long legs and she stared me hard. Then she took a sharp breath through her cigarette, and arched-up her left eyebrow at me with a bit of a sly smile. And I knew that I had a wing to sit under.

My mother whisked into town for a convention just as things were getting rolling. She took one look at me and trekked up to the Pharmaprix for protein powder and retin-A.

"Jesus, you look like a scurvied pirate, honey." I tried not to let that hurt my feelings.

Looking around the apartment, which I had spent a good while cleaning, her eyes welled up and her hands began to flutter around like two nervous birds. First there was the flipping of rings, the small spikes of light flashing over the walls. I wasn't sure what to do. Then came the rubbing of her hips, the flattening of skirt.

"Do-you-know-that-I-am-in-Real-Estate," she said finally, the words coming out of her mouth in that slow, articulated tone that means a person is somewhat on the verge of getting very upset. Then we had to leave.

"And don't be touching pay phones," my mother said.

"Gangs. They're putting rat-poison on the numbers now."

"It's a test," she said, swallowing a mouthful of chicken breast, "It's what you have to do to get in. Imagine."

She set her fork down a moment to shake her head.

"Honey, you're not eating."

I could feel the salmon fanning out inside of me before it had even left the plate.

"Jesus Gretchen. You look like you haven't had a decent meal in weeks. Come on honey, it's not everyday you get to eat at the Ritz."

"I'm not feeling well, Mom."

I wasn't. My body was a hovering dust catching in the upholstery.

"Of course you're not. It's not healthy to live in one room. I feel sick just thinking about it. Look, fly back with me tonight."

I watched her manicured hand slide across the table and onto another. There was no proof that it was mine.

"I can get you a job in reception by Tuesday."

Salty water was falling onto the dinner roll sitting in my skirt. Mom took a deep breath in and I was afraid of being swallowed.

"Honey, I know that you came here to prove that you can make things work, and you can. Your father and I both know that. But why here? And why a bakery for God's sake? We sent you to the ....four years of the..." she leaned forward in a forced whisper, her pupils knocking into me like two black marbles, *"Ashbury Girls do not work in bakeries."*

The silence rang between us like a chime along a long pipe. I thought about my uniform, still hanging in the closet like a dead duck. I'd burn it. Even dead ducks can fly back at you and bite.

"Ashbury Girls Go Forth With Grace and Knowledge. That was the motto Mom."

She tossed her napkin onto the table and leaned forward onto her elbows, clutching her own hands very tightly.

I hate it when my mother makes herself look so fashionably perplexed. It makes me feel like I'm on T.V., trapped in some very dramatic kind of show.

After a series of kisses, cash, arm rubs and a business card scrawled over in four numbers where she could be reached at any given time, Mom put me into a taxi. I wanted some space, some fresh air. I thought of getting out and walking once she had taken off in the other direction, but decided not to. I stuffed the fist full of bills into one pocket of my coat. Digging into another, I retrieved the lacey pastry paper and unfolded it beside me. The tooth rolled down the vinyl with a small clattering sound and onto the floor of the taxi. The driver didn't seem to notice, he was on about the weather. I hunched down closer to the carpeting, the mats wet and festery. The tooth shone in the dark like a small sabre. I picked it up and brushed it off, flipping it around in my fingers. Already I was feeling better. I spread my legs a bit to make a small hammock out of my skirt, and kept it there.

My reflection flickered up in the window. Parts of my face vanished in the shadows, the lights and the people and the street filtered through the rest, surfacing and resurfacing. I made a sort of wide grin at myself, then closed my mouth again quickly. I kept doing it, mesmerized. The white of my own teeth caught in the light and hovered over everything. The driver was talking to me. The price of gas, politics, or rain. I was having a hard time concentrating.

The night of the arcade, Serge had kept a fair distance until Hannah left to go buy a pack of smokes. As soon as she left, there he was, right back up next to me in his foul air. Though he spoke to me face-front this time, his words still hung in the air like warm, wet towels.

"She's trouble, you know. You can find better friends than her."

I turned away and sunk my knuckles into the bread dough, the nine grains scratching at my wrists.

"I worry about you, miss-s s-skinny bon-es," he said, back to the space between my ear and my head.

"If you ever need…"

Hannah plowed through the door.

"Goddamn Provigo, 4.60 a pack. Fucking ridiculous."

Serge ambled back to the counter and dumped a slab of ham onto the slicer. Hannah stood in the doorway and looked around sharply.

"Hey Gretchen," she said, her eyes on Serge, knowing, "Are you coming out with us tonight or what?"

I felt the red washing into me, my particles disbanding. Nothing.

"Gretchen, are you coming out with us or what?"

"Uh, yes, yes I will, am."

"Good."

She went back to cleaning the display. Fumes of No Name Fantastik filtered into the back room and Serge began pulling the pink ham hump over the blade. The pieces poured out. Little handkerchiefs of flesh.

I'm not sure if Hannah's boyfriend works at the arcade, I only know that he is there most of the time. That night, with my heart clamming up against my larynx, we made our way along Ste. Catherine to pick him up. I didn't know much about Jimmy.

"He's a bad bastard" Hannah had told me, "But I love him." When Jimmy opened the back door of the arcade he was not what I expected. He was skinny, a little gawky, with all sorts of moles dotting up his face and neck. I didn't think that bad bastards had moles at all.

"Babeee," he said, making a sultry sort of face at Hannah that was kind of funny.

"Who's this?" he said jerking up his chin a bit.

"Jimmy this is Gretchen, the girl from work. Gretchen, meet Jimmy."

I smiled in a weird sort of way with my teeth pressed into my lip.

"Hey," he said. "Baby, come say hi to the boys for a sec okay?"

"Alright." I could tell that they were sharing some kind of private joke.

"Gretchen, here, have a smoke, I'll be right back out." She handed me a pack of Player's and went inside, pulling the steel door shut with a slam. I looked around and tried to relax. The city was very quiet. 2 a.m. on a Tuesday night has a very nice quality about it. Even if you are standing in an alley behind some terrible arcade, you can appreciate the value of 2 a.m. quietness.

I'm not very good at the smoking. No matter how hard I try, I always feel like I'm sucking in the dustbin off a vacuum cleaner. Three drags and I knew it wasn't working out for me, and I bend down to put it out in the gray.

And there it was, cradled into a little dip in the snow. It took me a minute to realize. There was a bit of a brownish, thready matter on one end, but it came off easily enough when I ran my finger over it and rubbed it against my hand. It was heavy in my palm, like an anchor. It felt good.

There were a few tinny kicks at the door and I plunged the tooth under my jacket and into the kangaroo pocket of my sweatshirt. Hannah and Jimmy came out.

"Everything alright?" Hannah asked, looking from the hands in my pockets to my face, then back.

"Yeah."

And it was true. Somehow, suddenly, things were very fine.

Jimmy's apartment was above a bar with no name. It was nice enough, though it had that sort of man-sweat and smoke smell to it, and the couch was made of a green sort of burlap material that scratched. We had some apple-whisky popsicles made in that special Tupperware that lets you make your own, and we talked well into the morning. Well, Jimmy and Hannah talked mostly. I sat with my back against the couch, taking bitter licks of frozen whisky. I had one hand in my sweater the entire time. They didn't seem to notice, too busy recounting old times and slipping each others tongues down their throats. It was very interesting. The T.V. was singing O Canada and images of children and snow and sunflowers and dog sleds shimmered over their faces. The tooth fit into the pockets under my ribcage, my belly button, and could sit in between each of my collarbones as if resting in a bowl. My body was becoming more of a receptacle. Life no longer passed through me like a gust of spores.

When I got home, I dumped the rest of Mom's protein powder into a garbage bag and set it by the door. I ran a hot bath and slipped in, feeling work wash off me like a snake skin. Bread remnants and butter dots floated up to the line between water and air. My body hovered under, distending in the warm. I bit into my tongue a bit then ran it along the inside of my mouth. The medicine cabinet was open and from a certain angle I could see myself, a small slice in the tub. I was becoming sharp. There was a perimeter to me now, a series of pockets and dents under bones that cast shadows. I was there.

"I did it too," Hannah said to me one night, sitting out on the bread racks, the smoke weaving around us like a rope unraveling.

I was fiddling with the tooth, having sewn it into the hem of my t-shirt.

"Pardon me?" My voice was very small. I didn't want to share.

"I did it too, once, " she said "Stopped eating. It felt good."

I didn't know what to say.

"It's very Buddhist, you know. Cleansing and all that shit." She was staring me hard again. I clutched the hem of my shirt and smiled.

"Ya."

She turned away and threw a lot of smoke up into the air with her mouth.

"Just don't start puking. That's messed up. It wrecks your teeth, ya know. The bile."

She leaned her long back back up against the wall and rolled the ash of her cigarette into a point on the edge of the bread rack.

"Lose your teeth and you're gone. It's the only part of your body that lasts forever. Don't start with the puking."

I nodded. She flicked the cigarette back into the alley and we went inside.

That night, I gave Hannah my mom's credit card and felt good about it. She needed more things than I did. That's what I was feeling good about.

I remember Jimmy, wired on something and dancing to the golden-oldie tunes of a radio station from Vermont. They shrieked like monkeys and Jimmy's small body flung around the room. I watched for hours and laughed. Life was sweet. When I fell off into to sleep, I dreamt of my body floating over a discotheque, the hem of my shirt stretching and anchored to a floor full of light.

I don't know how it happened. I only remember Serge asking me to get the wheat flour from the cellar and the small steps. I know to be careful on those small steps.

I don't know how it happened.

When I came to, it was to the sound of Serge screaming at her, something about water and mops and lawsuits. I felt my cheek, at one with the cement step rather than my face. I was sharded out, a million bits soaking up the damp.

"It's not my fucking fault!" she said, throwing something into the wall of cake pans.

"Check her coat," Serge said, "There's got to be a number in there somewhere."

I cringed, my body fanning out in an blurry ache. I could smell the piney tile-grout water sloshing down the steps. It mingled with the red and pooled in my line of vision, floating three little white jags.

All that was left.

I closed my eyes and my hot, bloody jaw, wondering how many things I have ever bitten into with those teeth, how many things would bite into me now.

Daphne Marlatt

booking passage

> *You know the place: then*
> *Leave Crete and come to us*
> — *Sappho/Mary Barnard*

this coming & going in the dark of early morning, snow scribbling its thaw-line round the house. we are under-cover, under a cover of white you unlock your door on this slipperiness.

to throw it off, this cover, this blank that halts a kiss on the open road. i kiss you anyway, & feel you veer toward me, red tail lights aflare at certain patches, certain turns my tongue takes, provocative.

we haven't even begun to write... sliding the in-between as the ferry slips its shore-line, barely noticeable at first, a gathering beat of engines in reverse, the shudder of the turn to make that long passage out —

the price paid for this.

we stood on the road in the dark. you closed the door so carlight wouldn't shine on us. our kiss reflected in snow, the name for this.

under the covers, morning, you take my scent, writing me into your cells' history. deep in our sentencing, i smell you home.

there is the passage. there is the booking — & our fear of this.

you, sliding past the seals inert on the log boom. you slide & they don't raise their heads. you are into our current now of going, not inert, not even gone as i lick you loose. there is a light beginning over the ridge of my closed eyes.

passage booked. i see you by the window shore slips by, you reading Venice our history is, that sinking feel, those footings under water. i nose the book aside & pull you forward gently with my lips.

a path, channel or duct. a corridor. a book & not a book. not booked but off the record. this.

irresistible melt of hot flesh. furline & thawline align your long wet descent.

nothing in the book says where we might head. my tongue in you, your body cresting now around, around this tip's lip- suck surge rush of your coming in other words.

we haven't even begun to write... what keeps us going, this rush of wing-spread, this under (nosing in), this wine-dark blood flower. this rubbing between the word and our skin.

●

"tell me, tell me where you are" when the bush closes in, all heat a luxuri-ance of earth so heavy i can't breathe the stifling wall of prickly rose, skreek of mosquito poised... for the wall to break

the wall that isolates, that i so late to this: it doesn't, it slides apart — footings, walls, galleries, this island architecture

one layer under the other, memory a ghost, a guide, histolytic where the pain is stored, murmur, mer-*mere*, historicity stored in the tissue, text... a small boat, fraught. trying to cross distance, trying to find that passage (secret) in libraries where whole texts, whole persons have been secreted away.

original sin he said was a late overlay. & under that & under that? sweat pouring down, rivers of thyme and tuberose in the words that climb toward your scanning eyes

> *She shouts aloud, Come! we know it;*
> *thousand-eared night repeats that cry*
> *across the sea shining between us*

●

this tracking back & forth across the white, this tearing of papyrus cross-wise, this tearing of love in our mouths to leave our mark in the midst of rumour, coming out.

... to write in lesbian.

the dark swell of a sea that separates & beats against our joined feet, islands me in the night, fear & rage the isolate talking in my head. to combat this slipping away, of me, of you, the steps... what was it we held in trust, tiny as a Venetian bead, fragile as words encrusted with pearl, *mathetriai*, not-mother, hidden mentor, lost link?

to feel our age we stood in the road in the dark, we stood in the roads & it was this old, a ripple of water against the hull, a coming and going

we began with...

her drowned thyme and clover, fields of it heavy with dew our feet soak up, illicit hands cupped one in the other as carlights pick us out. the yell a salute. marked, we are elsewhere,

translated here...

like her, precisely on this page, this mark: *a thin flame runs under / my skin.* twenty-five hundred years ago, this trembling then. actual as that which wets our skin her words come down to us, a rush, poured through the blood, this coming & going among islands is.

in the current

"...one discovers the immense landscape ... of the passage.
— Hélene Cixous

isle isolé,
      pain enislanded,
                        i stand at your door, quick with
                              your here, my coming

pleasure on the rein leaps with anticipation, pleasure & grief so wound
                                                      together

It is the passage that can appear....

with anticipation of your opening, your light step to the door & the land-
      scape that unfolds its coastal curves, its rocks non-negotiable, its
      sudden isthmus isthmus oh
hello
      is most fragile for the mouth that connects

.   *...that can appear most difficult.*

i'm island, o stranded isolate that hesitates once more at a singular moun-
     tain (omitting mountains' joint footing underwater, o joined jouissant,
     the world is round she sang)

at your door the body in its forward motion trembles, *trans*-lated is(o *les
     oiseaux volants*

at your door — you open it, light flares in a great wedge from beyond
     your shoulders

          It happens in a flash. In a leap. Without transition....

welcome streaming out of your eyes. & risk. all the bodies we have loved
     pass their
shadows in transit between us

                    on the buoyant, in the current of a passage

impossible & yes, in trust

Oana Avasilichioaei

from Dragon

I

I fall into myth, a dragon belching laughter and vows.
I want to forget the sardonic grins of old-fashioned proletarians;
the mouth alive with the misery of orphaned wars, I choke
on the phlegm of a child's memory.
I am Dragon.
I scream.
Don't you recognize me? I am mountains and fields. Parades!

Last night I ate a peasant.
An alchemist at heart, he wanted me to mix cow milk, freshly squeezed, horse shit,
and a parsley leaf, spit flames and turn it into gold.
Instead I turned him in to the State.
Charged with blasphemy and conspiracy against the workers,
he saw his blue-eyed wife slowly starve and his few acres
join the collective farm.

I want to witness a *mortem profundam*.
Not a death that reeks of immortality, of aunts and fathers crying over pictures
smudged with the smell of Augusts spent at the summer cottage, or death
smeared with the colour of the tailor's skin when he spoke of babies at the
village wedding.
No.
I want death absolute, erased, complete.
No imprints, no etchings, memories, nothing.

Through the country I laugh and scourge, like an ocean scrubbing its
laundry with a tornado.
I am Dragon.
I scream.
Don't you recognize me?

The blue-eyed wife tried to bribe me, fed me cornmeal with red onions
and feta cheese.
Let me take a swig of slivovitz spiced with peppercorns and two swigs of
her breast.

I want my man back, she begged.
I tossed a bone and asked
Why want a man when you can have a Dragon?

She spat in my face, cursed profanities in the name of God and my genitals, so I grabbed
her wrists, squeezed just enough to see the veins bulge through her skin.
Listen, you wasted woman
I eat God.

A collector's burden

The train moves in small sobs
a loose anchor dragging on an ocean floor
a body with a shell instead of a swollen belly
and the roar of a conch instead of a throat.

The train moves
grinding rust off its weariness.
Through the window a scent of train lags;
thyme, oil and hot metal.

Skin sticks to plastic seats
an orange peel falls on the floor
everywhere the babble
of human sweat recoils.

See that woman in the corner
lurching with each movement of the train.
In that bag she hides people's used stories.
She will hide yours in exchange for your shirt.

Stephanie Bolster

Grade Seven

We didn't know in what way we were lost.
Each morning my jaw ached from the headgear
that wrenched my teeth across the gums

to make room for more. I glossed my chapped
lips with the pink of Bonne Bell bubblegum;
tried to feather my hair so the twin swoops met

at the back of my head: that spot only a mirror
or best friend could verify. My best friend
was a pen-pal on an island. I loved a fragile boy

and told him so, though he passed my note
to one boy and another, and soon enough
the whole class knew. One girl praised me;

the rest stared from their seats and mouthed
you? I couldn't become small enough
to be the dark-eyed Italian girl he chose for the slow

Valentine's Dance. In the photograph, our hair
hangs close about our faces; our leg-warmers and shoulders
slouch. Our lack of smiles was not an affectation.

I feared Junior High would shatter me into glass
fragments across the plush of tended lawns. No one
guessed I was that sharp. When I remember that time,

I envision myself in that snug bedroom
pillowed with unicorns, rainbows, and hearts,
as the slim bland girl in an American

novella, who didn't know how beautiful she was.
Really, the reason we felt ugly is because, just then,
we were. For once our vision of ourselves was accurate.

Things Buried in the Backyard

Each pet I've loved, except for those still living.
Roots of the living cherry tree and the dead,
roots of the neighbour's mock orange,
weed-roots. A massive toad
my father, digging to begin this garden
years before my birth, impaled by accident,
its cry sealed under several feet of soil
and the barberry bush. Probably those egg-shaped

Weebles we hid under cedar mulch
so we could unearth them later.
Possibly arrowheads, in the spot
where one surprised my young parents,
digging, and made them briefly imagine
being tracked in a dim place
of salal and swordfern. This dim place.
They hadn't imagined me. Who knows

how many earthworms, dewworms, cutworms,

leatherjackets, slugs, green pearls of slug eggs.
An excavation several centuries from now
would not unearth that toad's stabbed gasp
nor the moment when my father mentioned it,
then looked down at the nasturtiums,
and I saw he had lost something and I had not
stopped it, and I looked away.

rob mclennan

the darkness of that same century
(for diana brebner)

what thru the stony ground, elevates, a need
or consideration

it speaks to the same, what you think
you are thinking of

is this the best or the worst time for smalltalk

delivering messages to the nurse when yr
sound asleep, not
what a memory is for

this is still, & still a place for
what the heart goes out to

sharing a pack of earth, whether carrying
a satchel, or walks w/ a cane, still takes
the same #14 bus, still talks a while

we know where this is heading

& borders thru archways, the tremble
of past lives & present neath yr feet

& ishtar gate, astarte, the goddess of,
youd so long been searching, love

that together we might see more sky

it doesnt matter if you cant go home, you can
go back
to where you lived

four generations of a house set in, & the previous,
nothing left of it in the field

the garden knows a lot abt smoke, burning
matted grass each spring, thick grey

black is not the colour here

but when it is, so soon replaced
by short, green sprouts

Hal Niedzviecki

Korea

After, when this is all over, she'll be better for it.

It's just sex, she thinks.

Pleasure is distant, like a plane ride home.

She sucks her hands. Her hands smell like sperm.

Paula wakes up.

A foreign country.

It's a dream, a question, that is, of gradations, of habits and increments. If she isn't home, she isn't home.

What if she woke up back where she started? - wearing a paper uniform, frying potatoes in oil, serving them in thick cones of newspaper.

She isn't pretty like all the girls here must be pretty.

She gets out of bed because she has to. She pulls on a skirt, a blouse. She'll tell her class about oil spitting, summer jobs wearing orange pants that don't quite fit. It's about growing up. It's about learning another language. It's about going away a girl and coming home a woman.

She's teaching English to unblinking businessmen in ten minutes.

She checks her watch.

I love my mother, Paula thinks.

She thought she'd be back once a year, at least. Christmas. Or Thanksgiving.

The money was good, but she's a spender.

Then the currency dropped. Everything she had was worth nothing except for right where she was.

She's stopped eating.

She pushes herself through the streets, through stares like half moons settling.

So what? She's been out in the country, made love behind a bush with religious significance. The bugs here are different. Her father was old. She misses him.

Her hair is a mass of blond snakes.

One guy fucked her behind an ancient temple.

Check your watch.

French fries, she tells them.

She checks her watch.

On break, Lucy from Australia touches the pit of her back. Paula startles, spills thin brown gruel, their nasty version of coffee.

Tonight's the night, Lucy says.

Paula nods.

All the men want to have sex with her. They sit in the class room and imagine what it would be like.

She calls home.

It's me, she says lamely.

Oh my god. Honey. Paula honey. Is that you?

Her Mom sounds more enthusiastic then worried. It's one of those places where you go in and they give you a booth and you make your call. Paula hears the people in the booth next to hers, the octagon syllables. She's picked up a few simple words. She tries one out on her mother.

What? her mother said. What did you say?

It means Hello, Paula yells. Everybody in the phone place is yelling. Ten booths of relatives screaming over shoulders. It means, How are you?

Well isn't that nice, her mother laughs. I'm real fine honey. How are you? Honey I'm so glad you called. Everything's alright, isn't it?

Ah sure Mom. Everything's great here. Everything's fine. They play basketball here, and a game like dominoes only with more pieces.

Paula shifts the phone, throws the pill in her hand down her throat. She coughs.

What did you say, honey?

People want it all summed up. They want it funny and snappy and true to life. They have words here just like we do.

At the end of class she turns her back to them, scratches letters on the black board..

She talks while she writes.

Con-gra-tu-la-tions.

Con-kaw-chul-la-shons.

Thank you, she says.

It's funny how easy it is to just make things up. You tell them you're getting married. You tell them you're from Scotland. They shake your hand.

Once, two business men took you to a restaurant where a woman dressed in a black negligee fed each of you hot pieces of beef boiled in a spicy cabbage broth. This went on for hours. You weren't supposed to touch anything. If you picked up your glass to have a drink, she rushed over and grabbed it. The look on her face - like you stabbed her.

The two men sat on either side of you. You told them you were a heiress, that your father owned Disneyland, that you were thinking of their country as a future theme park site. You told them that back home you were maybe wanted for murder, but that your lawyers were working on it. They laughed, put their hands on your knees. You sucked a fruit that tasted like nuts, bit down on the server lady's finger. Her smile didn't waver. You went to the bathroom and swallowed two pills, they looked yellow in the light.

When you got back, the men were gone. The lady stroked her perfect hand through your tangled curls, gave you the bill. You could tell she felt sorry for you.

After school, Paula takes a taxi back to her one room apartment, even though it's only a five minute walk. She's shaking.

She's tried octopus and cuttlefish and sea weed. It was supposed to make her feel adventurous, but it just made her feel sick. At the bars, the men drink beer and gnaw on dried chunks of squid. Their breath smells like leather. Their faces get red. Their dicks are smaller then she's used to.

She's lies on her back in her underwear. Her chest in reluctant intervals. She's trying different ways to understand what's happening to her. The way it is versus the way it should be.

But nobody speaks her language.

I like being fucked in the ass.

She's eaten everything they've ever given to her. She's eaten jellyfish.

The girls walk fast, Paula is surprised that she's keeping up with them. They seem huge, compared to everyone around them. Paula's in the middle, all she can see is cleavage and elbows, all she hears are the clatter of heels on a shine smooth surface. They push through the doors to the banquet hall. Paula feels an anticipation in her, a light headed anxiety, as if anything could happen even though everyone knows exactly what's going to happen. It's like writing a letter home, she thinks. They tell you: take responsibility. They tell you: make a decision. A group of slate-faced men fuck you from behind, ties grazing the grooves of your spine. Later, they depreciate the currency. They fuck you, then shake your hand.

Her purse slaps against her hip.

She's in an evening dress, which doesn't surprise her.

If there was a ceremony, they've already missed it. Like always, people turn to stare. It's worse, because they're late. They stand at the back of the room, shy giggling giants. Paula checks her watch. Her wrist is bare.

On stage, a man does karaoke. Another man - the MC - wrests the microphone away, says something that makes the crowd laugh. All at once, they're surrounded by short men in tuxedos, their black hair shining in the light, patterned sequins snowing off the disco ball. Paula is offered a can of Budweiser. She accepts, lets herself be spirited away. The man laughs like he understands. Paula thinks about her class, feels a wave of tenderness for her group of blank faced businessmen, knows he doesn't understand. Everyone talks to her, shakes her hand. Paula drinks from a bottle of Heineken, swirls her tongue against the sour fizz. The men climb up on stage, belt out duets. The bride sits off to the side in a voluminous white dress. She smiles and avoids eye contact. She seems content. Then the MC again. Lights go out. Spotlights swirl. Paula feels a hand trail through her thighs. She closes her legs in a trap. A huge white cake floats on to the stage shooting firecrackers and trailing a cloud of smoke. The air is crinoline. Spot lights swirl. The bride bows in multiples, her single gestures slow and perfect. Everybody seems overjoyed, as if determined to carry on. Paula keeps putting a hand over her mouth, to make sure. The MC yells in another language. Fingers grazing the soft spots. Paula leans back, lets it happen, needs it to happen.

Then she's flying home, her mother has her in a bear hug.

So how was it? she wants to know. How was Korea?

She checks her watch. She's late for the funeral.

I've never been to Korea.

Carmine Starnino

Did You Say Your Prayers?

I did. Hands clamped, kneeling, I radioed my S.O.S.
into the coldest reaches of my six-year-old cosmos
and waited. They were simple prayers, standard distress
calls. Afterwards my bed became a listening post

homing in on every sound around me, the night's ceiling
sickle-mooned and starless. If it was a "step" that led
me closer to God, there was an evanescence to the feeling
prayer left behind: a wet footprint that soon started

to fade. Older, I learned to use the rosary, each tiny
bead I tweaked between my fingertips a spiritual
dollop I could measure. I prayed for friends, for family,
my every concern calculable, although miniscule

in its unit scale. I stopped that too. Each night I fussed
with a metaphysical ledger — how much I'd asked for
versus how much I'd given back. The rosary, an abacus
I grew tired of. But I've begun to miss it, prayer, or

maybe not exactly prayer, mostly just the suspense
of an answer. I like to think those childhood signals
still travel through deepest space, and if not his absence,
God's silence the reason I now count these syllables.

1955

The year Albert Einstien dies my mother is taught
to balance a jar of water on her head. She's great
at math, so when she dunks the jar into the well
I have her count each gulp as the clay belly grows

heavy in her hands. The year a UK team conquers
the Kanchenjunga in the Himalayas, the highest
unclimbed peak, the village boys take a tippy-toe
peek over the stone wall behind her, using a pile

of rocks to stand on. My mother lifts out the jar,
places it on the ledge, and while the BBC reveals
the world's first color TV, she pinches two opposite
corners of a white handkerchief, skipping-ropes it

into a long finger which she coils around the top
of her head as a cushion. Not exactly Marilyn Monroe
over a subway grating, her skirt huffing open
in an uprush of air, but for the boys enough to exceed

the imagination's 200 mph limit, like the record
Donald Campbell broke in his turbo-jet hydroplane
Bluebird. Yardbird? That's right, Charlie Parker
died too. I'd love to introduce some bebop into this,

trumpet and saxophone, a crazy tune each boy
improvises in his heart, as my mother crowns herself
with the jar, and climbs the hill home, keeping
level the concupiscence in their bodies, the water.

Melanie Cameron

"Just as every day"

Just as every day
someone I have never seen
comes to this corner
of the cemetery
beside the river,
shovel in hand,
and clears snow from a family
of graves, their flat
headstones, unable to stand
the thought of losing
his loved ones, yet
again, under this skin
of snow, as he has already
lost them beneath the skin
of death, I come

to this cemetery beside the river, not
because you are here – because you are
not, yet – but because this is where I find you

and me, arm in arm, like the trees rooted
to this eroding
bank, this is where I come
to stand each day
remembering
how deeply –
        so much more
        than six feet
        of earth, carefully turned, than
        the canal
        that births
        the Red, than
        the black-
        bird swooping
        down to meet the frozen body
        of this river
I love you

Kate Sterns

Excerpt from the novel *Down There by the Train*

To sharpen a sick man's appetite, and to restore his Taste
Take Wood or Garden Sorrel one handful, boyl it in a pint of white wine
Vinegar til it be very tender, strain it out, and put to it Sugar two ounces
and boyl it to a syrup and let the patient take of it any time.

Levon exited the diner at the exact moment a hockey player was being dragged off by his mother. The captain, square white teeth billowing out of his mouth like handkerchiefs on a clothesline, press-ganged Levon into replacing the missing teammate. Levon demurred, joking that his muscle definition was to be found only in the *Oxford English Dictionary*. The boys cajoled him into it, though, and he quickly amazed himself, and his team, with his considerable skills in the defensive position. His approach was to regard the net as the lungs of the game: skinless, exposed and vulnerable: a delicate interweaving of vein and artery, blood and oxygen pumping through them in a continuous circle (the manufacturer's stamp was even dyed in a red and blue pattern on the strings). All it took for a gaping hole to be made in it was a sixteen-year-old boy's attention to slip, and his foot with it. Levon understood the danger of that happening all too well.

He never knew what had gone wrong that afternoon. The weather was clear, no rain or fog. The intersection wasn't crowded; a good-bye kiss lasted longer than a stroll down the main thoroughfare of his small town. What had the boy been avoiding? A squirrel? A drifting leaf? His fate? He'd sworn his hand was firmly on the stick; he was alert and in control of the car, except for a brief moment when, for that unknown reason, he swerved. Levon recalled that he wore a snazzy pair of snakeskin boots; also, that he'd managed to walk away from the accident in them. The boy was sorry, of course he was *sorry*, but by then it was too late; Alice's lungs were punctured. She was bleeding internally.

There seemed to be a dispute about the scoring. Levon consulted with the player closest to him, a boy with sandy hair and black roots, like an oil slick on a beach.

—Overtime, he explained. Sudden death.

Levon glanced reflexively at his watch. Noon. The two hands clapped together, reminding him to get going. The January sky was a pasty white veined with leafless treetops. There would be little enough light as it was. Ceremoniously, he proffered his stick to his captain. Levon was tempted to quote from Homer but knew he'd be asked what team Homer played on, and what position, and what his number was. His number was up. Now the Greats wore skates.

Warmed up after his unaccustomed exertions it wasn't until Levon had strolled the ten or so blocks south to the lakeshore that he realized how chilly the air was, and how inadequately he was dressed for crossing the ice. A lake breeze caused his blue serge trousers to pulse against his leg like a vein. *In the parts the blood is refrigerated, coagulated, and made as it were barren.* The damp air seeped through the thin lining of his jacket. The fact that the island appeared to be much further off than he'd calculated added to his worries. Furthermore, it was wrapped in a shroud of mist, sewn, no doubt, by the ghosts of those long dead tailors.

He chose as his starting off point a section of the waterfront where the land sloped gently down, merging with the frozen lake and presided over by a modern sculpture—two enormous intersecting aluminum rectangles— which no one had liked at first. Waste of money! Too abstract! Why not a historical figure astride a horse? *That* had worked for centuries. People had grown used to it, though, and even proud of it. Familiarity breeds art, perhaps, and not contempt. He had forgotten the sculpture was called *Time* but so it was. An appropriate launching place for this new phase of his life.

The ice felt reassuringly firm underneath his shoes although he was intrigued to discover as he walked (tiptoed more like) that the ice close-up was not white, which was how it looked from shore, but a mottled purple and black, like a bruise. Nature was as fragile as a human being. Indeed,

Sweeney's final warning, issued in a sonorous voice, still resounded in Levon's ears:

—A woman don't melt as fast as the ice sometimes does.

Each winter, the local newspaper reported the death of an islander who , either inebriated or too impatient to get home, gunned his truck over the frozen lake and, midway across, hit a weak spot in the ice. Levon imagined the driver scrabbling frantically to unlock his door as frigid water bubbled up from below, perhaps assuming the shape of the Harpies: fierce-looking women, the curve of the waves their breasts, the stench of seaweed and rotting fish clinging to the spume of their hair. Released from their dank cave, the hags would drape themselves over the sinking automobile, surround the hapless driver and drag him screaming down, down, down to the underworld. Hadn't there been three? *Aello*, storm. *Ocyptete*, rapid, and a third. Who was the third? Ah, yes. *Celeno*. Darkness. A storm, and then rapidly, darkness. That was death and also, life lived in the shadow of a death.

Levon did not relish becoming an item in *The Gazette*, that grubby, gossipy rag. He pictured his obituary, a column the shape of a coffin, framed in mournful black ink. Levon Hawke, *troublesome* son of Mr. and Mrs.Thomas Hawke of Muckfoot, Alberta; devoted brother of Alice, *now deceased*. Drowned. Silly bugger tempted Fate. *Serves him right*.

He pressed on as speedily as he could.

No skaters were out but there remained on the ice strokes in the shape of apostrophes, commas and parentheses cut by blades earlier in the day. The blank surface of the ice was edited into paragraphs, sentences, subordinate clauses, fragments, words: Lost, hypothermia, arctic, Shackleton, fool, no, hero, Scott, idiot, no, misguided, frostbite, amputation, slippery, perish, uncertain, frightened, heart, diastole, systole, shit, falling, falling, falling, *fuck*.

His knees bashed against the ice, his chin, his elbows too. Pain lurched through him, down this corridor and that, like a drunk who's forgotten where his bed is until, at last, it came to rest, reeling and nauseated, in the pit of Levon's stomach.

Cautiously, he rolled over on his back. He expected to hear the jangle of coin-sized bones within the loose pocket of his skin. No. No bones broken. What about the ice? Had he detected a shift, a slight bobbing underneath his shoulder blades? He thought all at once of cartoons; of how one character in pursuit of another would be lured to a patch of thin ice and would then watch it crack in zig-zagging lines around him until he was perched on an ice floe. Facing the screen, the cartoon figure sank slowly, resignedly, into the water only to emerge unscathed on shore in the next frame, calmly wringing out his entire body as though it were a dishrag; first his feet twisting around and around, then his legs followed by his torso, his neck, his head and even his ears. He squeezed out every drop of moisture apart from tears. The cartoon character never cried. His response to adversity was anger and a wily, although inevitably disastrous, revenge.

No again. He and the ice were both intact. Frozen solid, in fact.

The pain dulled to a thud in his patella and olecranon. Still he couldn't bring himself to shift. Levon watched in groggy fascination as a she-moon, hovering above him like the blade of a scythe, cut down the feeble winter sun, which tottered, scattering a few drops of blood on the horizon, before falling to the ground. *Celeno* and *Ocyptete*. The hour couldn't have been much past three o'clock in the afternoon, if that. Night, snow, the world was falling about Levon's ears. Stretched out on that gurney of ice, growing stiffer by the second, Levon could almost feel the whistle of the moon's blade as it swung, preparing to open him up for dissection. He trusted it was William Harvey's hand which held the blade over him and not God's. The doctor, at least, had a practical use for his dead. Harvey had cut into the living, too; dogs, though, not humans. He had wanted to examine their still beating hearts.

When I first applied my mind to observation from the many dissections of Living Creatures as they came to hand, that by that means I might found out the motion of the Heart and things conducible in Creatures; I straightways found it a thing hard to be attained, and full of difficulty, so with

Fracastorus I did almost believe, that the motion of the Heart was known to God alone.

Not that Harvey was fazed by this. Not at all. He continued to poke and speculate, reason, experiment and sometimes kill in order to understand how the human organism worked. Autopsy meant 'to see for oneself' and Levon wanted to. He wanted to know, for example, why he remembered that passage (learned by heart as it were) and yet, had forgotten so much of what was truly important: the name of Alice's first boyfriend, the part she'd acted in the school play, her favourite fairytale: the subject she and Levon were arguing about when she stepped, just ahead of him, onto the street. He was curious about what this jumble inside him looked like. Oh, he'd examined all the anatomist's drawings: the medieval representations of a man split from neck to pubis, a bottle shaped opening in which his organs resembled the glops and squiggles left by an ineptly squeezed tube of paint; the Renaissance skeleton posed in mid-gambol as though its skin had blown off in a fierce wind; William Hunter's gruesome detail of a pregnant woman's womb, the trunks of her legs cut off mid-thigh as a butcher would a joint of beef. Levon's anatomy was undoubtedly of the standard variety but he felt a close kinship with the eccentric renderings of earlier times, when humours and spirits were believed to be as essential a component of the body as were blood and bones and tendons. Laid out in a neat, geometric pattern, a square within a tilted square, were the four humours—choleric, melancholic, sanguine and phlegmatic—their corresponding elements—fire, earth, water and air—poised at the angles. Levon pictured his own insides as being less ordered than that; more a child's finger painting with chaotic streaks of black and yellow bile merging with sanguine blood.

Aello.

Enough, the wind hissed, icy fingers sliding underneath his back and pushing him into an upright position. Move, the sharp edge of the moon threatened him. Run, thundered his heart, run *now*. But in which direction? He had tripped while a little more than half way across the ice judging from the distance of the city, which he sat facing. It was dotted with rouge—an artificial, rosy light—and the cheeriness of it beckoned to him. Levon knew it was fake, knew it would be wiped off in the cold, creamy light of morning. For now, though, the city represented the land of the living. The island, on the other hand, was barely discernible. A cluster of lights shone from what he assumed was the ferry dock. The rest was pitch.

Cool, minted air cracked between his chattering teeth. A grating wind shred curls of snow all around him. He brushed them from his hair and shoulders as others melted, trickling down his neck and along his spine, cold as the anatomist's knife sectioning him off. His pace became quicker. He ought to have refused Simon's offer, or at least waited until morning. A new life requires labour but this stumbling about in the gloom, not knowing how far off he was from the shore, or in what condition he would arrive, *if* he did at all? That was more like death than birth.

For comfort, Levon touched the pocket in which he carried Sweeney's parting gift, the o, a talisman. Think of that, he commanded himself: a letter can change everything.

God became good.

Alice became alive.

What, he wondered, would Simon's letter change?

For an hour or more he walked. The snow grew progressively deeper; first cushioning his soles, then slopping over his shoe tips and, at last, swirling around his ankles. This meant there must be a barrier here from the bristling wind that, in the centre of the lake, swept the surface clean of snow. His eyes played a game of tag with the island, dodging left and right, trying to catch sight of it and so, be able to shout *home free!* He thought he spotted a vague outline of tall, ghost-white shapes looming ahead, their arms waving, teasing him, challenging him to approach. At the same time, his ears picked up a low-pitched moaning punctuated by shrieks and whistles.

He stumbled forward, arms outstretched. A few minutes later, he felt a vicious jab against his palms.

A pine branch? Spruce? Squinting into the darkness, he supposed the paler forms might be birch, or beech. In truth, Levon didn't know his ash from his elm tree. Sweeney hadn't mentioned trees at all. The map he'd drawn for Levon resembled nothing so much as a boot, the toe pointed in a well-aimed kick towards him as he crossed the ice. The blow connected, sharply, as he stepped on shore.

Unwilling to step back on to the ice, even to follow the shore around to a clearer spot, he decided to brave the woods. As a child, he'd been an avid reader of fairytales and, to a degree, his work in medical history began as an extension of his childlike delight in narrative. History was part story, after all. Levon's imagination loosely transposed the physician as hero, ignorance for the woods, and disease for the dragon. It didn't hurt, either, that damsels occasionally swooned in the doctors' arms. However. Faced with the prospect of an actual wood, in which actual wolves might roam, his nerve wavered. He did not want to be mistaken for a thing with feathers.

He had no choice it seemed. Gritting his teeth, he grasped a low hanging branch further ahead, at the same time letting go of the first one, and pulled himself forward. He repeated this action, partnering himself off as though at a square dance, and in this manner, made gradual, clumsy progress among the trees.

Snow muted his footfalls. Levon heard nothing but his hoarse breath and, once, the purr of wings in the distance. This silence was unheard of in prison. There it was never quiet. An inmate shouted at his neighbour to quit talking, another raised the volume of his radio to drown out the shouting. The next man thumped on his bars to signal that the radio was too loud. A guard yelled. A door clanged shut. Toilets flushed. It was thuggish noise, noise that loitered at corners and bullied passers-by, battering them, robbing them of their wits. But the woods were filled with the purposeful, respectful silence Levon remembered from the library, enforced by a librarian's gentle *shhh* as branches stirred at his touch. Blindly, he went on, his finger tips brushing over tree bark, a kind of braille, the meaning encoded in a text that was unfamiliar to him. What was he to learn here?

He grew intensely aware of the darkness without as well as within him. Would he ever see light again? For almost three years he'd lived with the continuous illumination from bulbs dotting the corridor, their sulphurous yellow glow encased in wire mesh, as if light, too, could be imprisoned. An inmate was not allowed even his own shadow for fear of what he might do under its protection. Daybreak was just that: a broken day, unfixable, worthless, indistinguishable from night.

Given the absence of a real, discernible shape on which to focus, a horrible idea began instead to take shape in Levon's mind. He tried to shake it off but it stuck nonetheless. His sense of geography was weak and, after all, there had been no signposts, no illumination of any sort.

What if he had landed on the wrong island?

Thousands of them littered the lake. Ancient relics of a giant crack-up of the earth's surface. Some were no bigger than a tea cup while others, like this one, were more substantial. The majority of them, he thought, were further east, or was it west? In which direction was he headed? On what side of a tree did moss grow? Did the north star really shine from the north or was it a trick, like the question about who lies in the tomb of the unknown soldier? And which way was north anyway? He couldn't start a fire from striking two rocks together, or construct a shelter from twigs or track an animal, let alone kill it. He had never enjoyed *Boy's Own* stories and, while fairytales were chock full of adventures as exciting as any schoolboy might wish, the advice offered in them was not exactly practical. Elves weren't likely to spring out at him from behind a tree bearing magic hawthorn branches or golden apples or a pair of seven league boots.

No, what appeared to Levon at that moment was far more astonishing than that. He rubbed his eyes, almost scraping off the cornea with his knuckles, as if underneath the image reflected there was another, truer one if only he could get at it.

A house.

In the middle of the woods.

The sickle moon had been hard at work here, clearing trees to form a semi-circle of land in which the house, tall and angular, stood brooding. As Levon stepped forward, half-expecting the house to dissolve in a whirl of snowflakes, a bony branch hooked his collar, yanking him back. He unsnagged himself, impatient to be free of the splintery wood. Whatever was ahead couldn't be nearly so frightening, or unfriendly, as what lay behind.

The house slept, its windows shuttered. There was a faint creaking sound, as of an old woman shifting in her corset. Levon's fingers probed knotted strands of ivy, lifeless and unkempt, that spilled down the walls. Icicles dripped from a snowy gable, a deserted bride's tattered hat and veil. A gnarled oak tree, thick around the middle, rapped insistently—tip,tap,tip-Con a shutter, a suitor in disgrace begging to be let in, to explain matters and to be forgiven.

Dazed, Levon drifted with the snow up to the front door. He picked up the ornate, brass dragon knocker. Determined to observe the proprieties, despite the silliness of announcing his arrival at a house which had been deserted, clearly, for months, if not years, Levon listened to the reverberations fade without hearing any answering footsteps from inside.

He did not notice the brief lick of candlelight along the slat of a shutter. He was unaware of the shadowy cameo of a girl pinned to the inside wall, her profile regarding him in blank surprise.

He did not hear her sharp intake of breath, which, Levon might have convinced himself, was the wind threading itself through the iron filigree.

Levon leaned his forehead against the doorjamb, confused about what he ought to do. He had broken and entered once before. No. He'd been broken-hearted and *then* entered. Not that the law recognized such a distinction. Anyway, merciless Nature was both Judge and Jury here. Wearing its black robe and snowy wig, it was Nature who would pronounce sentence upon him: a minimum of frostbite: the maximum penalty, pneumonia or even death.

I had no choice, your Honour.

His fingers trembled so badly he could scarcely grasp the door knob.

It turned easily.

John K. Samson

Liminal Highway

when you fall asleep in transit
you rarely wake up much closer
to where you want to be
and you've missed the song
you were waiting to hear
coming up after the ad for a
funeral home and the traffic and weather
in a town you'll never live in

or even see now that you've passed it
in a dream you don't recall

and you know there is a word
for those seconds between
consciousness and sleep where you
have arrived at your destination
accomplished your tasks and
concurrently settled into a
big old house that needs some work

next to the funeral home
with some endlessly interesting and
kind person you love unflinchingly

and traffic is moving well
weather is fair

you think that word might be "liminal"
but you are not certain so you don't
mention it to the driver who's name
you cannot remember

though you likely know him
as well as you know anyone

and you are so weary
with loitering between here
and there then and then
beauty and function you wish
you were a three hole punch
sleek shiny black and a
mysteriously pleasant weight
assisting children with their
school presentations while

slowly stockpiling confetti
for no particular occasion

just some average day
suddenly it is needed

Manifest

I want to call requests through heating vents
and hear them answered with a whisper "No."
To crack the code of muscle, slacken, tense,
let every second step in boots on snow

complete your name with accents I can't place
that stumble where the syllables combine.
Take depositions from a stranger's face.
Paint every insignifigance a sign.

So tell me nothing matters, less or more,
at all, say "Whatever it is we think actions are,
we'll never know what anything was for."
If "Near is just as far away as far,"

and I'm permitted one act I can save,
I choose to sit here next to you and wave.

Julia Tausch

Selections from *Gepäckträger*

In Paris she sees Diane Arbus photos for the first time at the Georges Pompidou centre in Paris and they are it and she writes it all down, what a stupid fool writing down pictures, right there all alone in Paris in the ridiculously architectured Georges Pompidou centre. The escalators are on the outside, and she's writing down pictures in Paris alone and later she eats yoghurt, a cup of yoghurt costs five dollars here where the escalators are on the outside but for that you can look down on the giant hamburger in the beginning of the gallery or can you I can't quite remember and she eats the yoghurt and it's in a glass jar so you can see the fruit on the bottom right there on the bottom before you even stir it up and the yoghurt is so fatty and so good because it's Europe, will she ever be able to eat Canadian yoghurt again, without a sharp pang without a word of remorse, (and the answer is no, she's a yoghurt snob, it's a runny mess) and she reads over what she wrote what she frantically scribbled on a little small pad of yellow paper with her Tate Gallery pen, her Tate Gallery bubble pen, the one where the Lady of Shallot floats down the river to her death, right there in the pen: Yetta Granat is 72 and Charles Fahrer is 79. They have never met before. 1970. That is all. They have never met before, these are the winners, king and queen of the senior citizens' dance in Yonkers New York and there it is, that's really as good as it gets, there it is, writing down a picture for God's sake, what a stupid—and they're both wearing crowns and they both look pissed off and Charles has a sceptre and a cloak—fool. That was the same day she sat alone in the Joseph Beuys room I think, a whole room, a little room, but a whole one papered, not papered, with thick brown puffy insulating stuff, a fool to write down stuff, the stuff he always makes stuff with this ridiculous artist this ridiculous man an artist, he puts rolls of the stuff in corners too but this time he papered NOT papered—a whole room with it and she went into it and she had to duck down a bit to get through the door and that's part of the fun for sure so it's part of the art for sure and no one else was inside so she had a seat because you couldn't hear anything. You couldn't hear Paris and you couldn't hear the escalators grinding up and down on the outside and when you couldn't hear those things then maybe just maybe the other side fell away too, sometimes, just sometimes home stopped talking inside your head and when home stopped talking inside your head maybe just maybe you weren't thinking about driving to the movies in Ben's car with the showtunes going and Sabrina in shotgun and you in the back and maybe you weren't thinking about stupid Robert and his stupid new girlfriend and maybe just maybe all you were thinking about was that you are the luckiest luckiest girl who ever lived to be sitting in this small, whole room papered, oh, with thick brown puffy insulating stuff that's art even, listening to nothing at all. Maybe she wasn't allowed to sit on the floor here she wasn't sure, so when more people came in she got up right away, right away, little red guilt dots burning on both cheeks.

•

In Seville in the south of Spain during the Semana Santa a girl is remembering a boy who loves alliteration. It's a beautiful night. It's hot outside, pouring rain. On Thursday nights here, everyone goes to a store near the main square that sells liquor and dozens of smoked hams hang from the ceiling, pointing their small two-toed feet. They have little plastic cone shaped cups attached to their bottoms, to collect the dripping grease. And everyone young orders a Loté. Sarah and Tim just yell the word because their Spanish is horrible and they're drunk already from the sangria at dinner. Loté! Gin! Fanta Limón! And it all comes in a plastic bag, two twenty-sixers of gin, two big bottles of lemon pop, four plastic cups, a big bag of ice, fifteen bucks, let's get this show on the road is what Tim says and Sarah laughs and can't believe he used such a dorky expression and can't understand why she isn't madly in love with him.

They go and find the others, standing under an awning, smiling big and ready. Tomorrow the gang goes to Morocco on the six am bus so the plan is to drink till then and sleep on the way. The plan is foolproof. They'll wake up in Africa and the word alone makes them afraid of what they'll do or say wrong, makes them drink the gin quicker than they have to, makes them know each other better than ever before. And the climax comes when they run into goddamned Germans who literally are everywhere buying litros of beer once all the gin is gone. Sarah drops her bottle as soon as Tim places it in her hand and it's the funniest thing that's happened to either of them as long as they have lived and she hugs him around his waist from behind and he puts his hands on hers and they decide to go back to the hostel and have just an hour long nap. Cory and Ann do the same. Meet at five am in the square is the word and they go stumbling through the streets. And Sarah and Tim hold hands and are lost and they pass the street San Roberto four or five times and every time Sarah says something but she can't remember what she's said three minutes after she says it. It takes them two or three hours to walk the ten minutes back to the hostel and they sleep soundly through the alarm. At ten am they go to bang on Cory and Ann's door in the vain hope that they're not in Africa either. And sure enough they spent the night puking, first on each other, then one in the toilet, the other in the bidet, high romance.

It isn't until the next day when they finally catch a bus to the sea that Tim reams Sarah for calling him Robert the whole night they held hands.

•

When my father was five years old he puked on a ship for three weeks flanked by his older brother and his older sister, also puking. For three weeks. And my Grandmother had to oversee the whole thing. Between pukes of her own naturally. Holding hair back for her five, seven and eight year-olds, my Grandmother did not have a lot of time to get excited about the great white adventure that awaited. My father, at the age of five, was not excited in the least, nor was he discontent. He would vomit then drift off to sleep dreaming of the pigs on the farm, the farm that had been his home until the ship. He'd dream about days spent poking pieces of straw into the pigs' moist, quivering nostrils. He'd dream about the deep blue sea and he'd dream about Canada that his mother and father had been talking about lately and appeared to his subconscious mind to look something like a fried egg but larger, a fried egg you could stand on. He liked the way their berth made the whole family sleep in same sized beds. His parents didn't get a big bed on the ship like they did on the farm. Everybody in the same little bed with blue sheets and blue blankets to match the sea that just kept going and going for hours and days and weeks on end, heaving his little tummy up and down in time with his little bed and his older brother and his sister and his parents too. The ship made everybody the same.

And then there was a party. There was a big fat party with music, German music with accordions and lots of beer and singing and laughing and his mother, my Grandmother cried, finally, after three weeks of holding hair back and holding tears back and holding my father's hand when he was afraid she finally let it go. My father's older sister got a lesson that night that you could cry about happy things too, that's what my Grandfather told her. That my Grandmother was so happy that they were finally there, finally in Canada that she was crying tears of joy. My Grandfather didn't cry. He danced and danced and drank and sang in German until the sun cracked through the sea and took over the sky.

Of course I've imagined some of this, I wasn't there, I don't know that my Grandmother cried necessarily and I don't know that she hadn't for the three weeks before the big fat party. But that's roughly how it happened, my father's trip from Germany to Canada, to Toronto where he's lived pretty well ever since, where he met my mother at a bar one night when he was out to get drunk and smoke cigars all by himself. My mother who had come all alone in a jet plane, over the sea that just kept going and going for minutes and hours and she watched every second. She watched even the black window until the sun turned the sky gold and the sky shook and spilled my mother's drink but she didn't mind because she'd already had four and they had all been included in the price.

•

Hannelore is 65 years old and before she flew to London that bright day in May, she had never in fact left Germany. But on that bright day in May she got into a taxicab and the air smelled different. It was a cold smell, it had been a cold May, but that wasn't all. There was another smell, a bit like metal. She imagined that she could already smell the plane, but that was stupid and then she imagined that she could smell adventure and desire, but really that was stupider. And when she got there, to the Stuttgart airport, there they were, all those students in their twenties. Early twenties. In light spring coats, hair loose and dyed, not out of necessity but as an adventure. And Hannelore stood at the fringe of the group and smiled a warm smile and waited. And when she was mistaken for a professor, she didn't know quite what to feel but she certainly didn't feel proud. And when she said that she was a student and she was here for the English department field trip to Stratford upon Avon, they all smiled funny. A bit embarrassed. A bit confused. When the lights snapped up in The Other Place theatre and the actor from the movie Howard's End that Hannelore had recently seen the dubbed version of on cable TV started telling her that he has been studying how he may compare this prison where he lives unto the world, Hannelore was pleased that they'd chosen fluorescent lighting for this particular production because it was much easier that way to read along. She'd found a handy-dandy section in a darker corner of the mega-bookstore beside the McDonald's in tiny sleepy Tuebingen, little no-frills paperback Shakespeares with the English on one side of the page and the German right there on the other. Each just eight marks fifty. She'd bought one of each of the plays they'd be seeing on the field trip, and was happy that each had a different coloured cover. She decided not to read them before the trip, so as not to ruin the story. She would simply use them as a helper when the English got a little tough. So when the fluorescent lights snapped up, though it was not the lighting she was expecting from the Royal Shakespeare Company, Hannelore couldn't have been more pleased. She placed her little yellow edition of King Richard the Second on her knee, held it open with one hand, just far enough away from her bifocals that the words were sharp as tacks. They'd learned earlier on their backstage tour organized by the English department that over sixty per-cent of the Royal Shakespeare Company's audience each night was comprised of folks who spoke English as a second language. She was just thinking to herself that she was likely the only one in the theatre smart enough to have brought along her own personal set of subtitles and for only eight marks fifty. Smarter than all of the other students, students who were the right age and would discuss the right things at the Dirty Duck pub after the show because they'd studied each play months in advance and ruined the story and everything. And then Bolingbroke stole her thunder. More literally, less dramatically, he stole her book, clear off her knee, right out of her hand, from under her bifocals and began to read out loud from the script. From the English side. A lucky thing Hannelore was following diligently or he might have got all muddled up.

And when she walked away from the students and their dyed hair and their carefully ordered pints she meant to go to the bathroom and then back to the guest house. Maybe watch a little English TV. Maybe drink some of the tea included in the price of the room. Instead she walked right on up to him in the Dirty Duck pub at 10:30 PM, his eyebrows still caked with makeup, and Henry Bolingbroke gave Hannelore an autograph and she gave him a loud, clear thank you. In English. There didn't seem to be much more to say.

•

"Well, one of my more memorable moments was when we did this very modern Hamlet, you know, all updated and everything, and so of course we had Ophelia die by drug overdose, of course, and the director just had to, I mean come hell or high water, just had to have her vomit on stage. It was his last show with the company and everything and it was his baby and he, I can still remember him coming up to me and just begging me to think of a way to let Ophelia vomit on stage and I said alright, alright, let me have a look at the set and everything, and all of the sudden I had this great idea. And so there I am, opening night, all in my blacks, just *praying* that I don't botch this up, it was after all, my great idea, so it had better work right? And I'm there, underneath the stage you know, and we've got this sewer grate sort of thing on stage where the top of one of the trapdoors usually is, you know what I mean? And I'm under there, where the trap-door leads, with a big syringe, like a big turkey baster sort of a thing really all full of vanilla custard, and I have to wait for Ophelia to come stumbling and reeling over the grate thing, because she's just overdosed of course. And when she kneels down over the grate, and it's all very dramatic, the lighting and everything, I shoot the turkey baster right into her mouth, and she sits right up and spits custard up all over herself, and of course right back down through the grate onto me, into my hair and everything. Of course I asked if we could use soup, you know, get a bit of a clear vomit effect, with just a few chunks, but no, that's no good because our Ophelia gets so caught up in the moment that she's terribly upset and she needs comfort food. So what can I say, of course dear, would custard do, and it did, and so we did it that way. I mean, you have to deal with them, the actors because really, they're what make the show. Well, them and Shakespeare of course. But anyway, well. I guess the point of that whole story is that I have one of those jobs where I wake up in the morning and I just can't wait to go. I love my job. I think I probably have the best job in the whole world. Are there any questions?"

And I am just so inspired by all of this, I just can't believe it, and I've written down the key points of every anecdote she's told into my little small pad of yellow paper and I'm looking around at all the Germans with me on this field trip to Stratford, sad for them that they may have missed the finer points of this wonderful wigmaker's motivational monologue and I write that down, too, a recent sucker for alliteration. Looking around at all the Germans, I can't help but look at Hannelore. Hannelore who's sixty-five and was mistaken for a professor when we all met at the airport. Hannelore, her notebook sitting in her broad, brown lap, the open page empty except for the date in the upper right-hand corner. I feel like shaking her, I don't know why, for having missed this, it makes me so mad. I think I probably have the best job in the whole world! Hello! Hello Hannelore, how can you sleep through something that beautiful and poetic and true and she just sits there like an old, brown mountain, hadn't been on a plane before two days ago and while everyone's trumpeting her glory, and their pride in her I want to shake her and make her see, really see. What? She probably won't take another plane after the one that takes us back to Stuttgart, she already told us that. And everyone told her that's ok, at least she's had this one adventure. A week-long adventure away from her husband and their dog and her fridge stuffed with cheese and eggs and butter and her freezer crammed with red meat and hard, heavy bread. The whole class, the whole world is sitting around on their uncomfy chairs asking inane questions and Hannelore is making a breathing whistle in her sleep and I close my small little pad of yellow paper and put it back into my bag.

Sarah Steinberg

Telling the Difference: Michael Vs. a Crocodile

This is a jackhammer with a fixed centre. Fact: Crocodiles don't make omelets in my kitchen on football Sunday and flip back and forth between the game and me and the Discovery channel. They don't cook omelets in my kitchen and use up three of my eggs, leave dirty dishes in my sink, filled ashtrays and unwrapped zucchini which I told you would go bad if it wasn't wrapped up and

Think astronomy,
think planets turning on their axis

crocodiles don't flip back and forth between football Sunday and make-out Saturday and drunken Friday and flip back and forth between bringing me salad and berating me in the kitchen and making an omelet, such a dainty food thing, and asking me too many questions, berating me between flip back and forth between

This is a corkscrew, ripping into the neck of the bottle,
turning, spinning, swirling into the body of the wine.

running your hands up my legs my thighs my feet on your legs
flipping back and forth between massages and foul language between me
or the TV between the sheets between then and now they don't fall in love
and then out between now and then they don't call at four in the morning

and a steering wheel, including the hands of the driver

ask if they can come over, then not and apologize later,
then do it again. They make no pretence about the cut of their teeth. They
don't cook their meat.

A fulcrum.
A pirouette.

Moving Across a Frozen Surface

Mother drops me off in front of the arcade.
She groans and gropes around in the back
of the car: my hat, my mitts, my scarf.
Don't you dare take those off, she says,
I don't care what your father is wearing.
I swing my skates over my shoulder, I slam the car door.

My father sits behind the change booth,
he makes quarters for the players
and on his break he plays Ms. Pac-Man.
He is an addict.
He sees me and hugs me; I can smell the camel cigarettes on his cheeks
the sweat and denim, coffee and grass, and other mysteries.

Men call to him on the street.
He stops them, he grasps my shoulders.
This is my daughter, he says.
This is my daughter. He says my name
and there is always an extra r inside it.

It is some part of his Brooklyn past
he can't get out of his mouth.
He buys me a hot chocolate,
pays mostly in quarters.

The pond at the park at Yonge and Gould has frozen over.
There he sits, shivers, smokes and fidgets,
as I make small circles around the boulder in the middle of the ice,
sometimes falling over.

Contributors

ROBERT ALLEN is a novelist and poet. His most recent books are *Ricky Ricardo Suites* (poems) and *Napoleon's Retreat*, a novel, both published by DC Books, Montreal. His long poem, *The Encantadas*, will appear in 2003 with Signal Editions, Vehicle Press, Montreal. He is the editor of the literary review Matrix

OANA AVASILICHIOAEI's "Dragon" and "A collector's burden" come from a book length project entitled *Abandon*, which deals with a dictator, a dead woman and a sleepy town in Romania. Oana now lives and works in Montreal, where she will be delving into the next book which is about a park and a snake charmer. Some of her work has appeared in Prism International, Antigonish Review, Matrix and an anthology entitled *Running with Scissors* (Cumulus Press).

STEPHANIE BOLSTER has published three books of poetry: *White Stone: The Alice Poems* (Governor General's Award and Gerald Lampert Award, 1998); *Two Bowls of Milk* (Archibald Lampman Award and Trillium shortlist, 1999), and *Pavilion* (2002).

ROB BUDDE has published three books: *Catch as Catch* (poetry, Turnstone 1995), *Misshapen* (novel, NeWest 1997) and *traffick* (poetry, Turnstone 1999). He edits an ezine called stonestone at stonestone.unbc.ca. He is still uncertain what he wants to be when he grows up but currently teaches creative writing and critical theory.

MELANIE CAMERON is the author of *Holding the Dark* (poetry, 1999, J. Gordon Shillingford Inc.), which was shortlisted for the Eileen MacTavish Sykes Award for Best First Book by a Manitoba Writer. Melanie was shortlisted for the John Hirsch Award for Most Promising Manitoba Writer in both 1999 and 2001. She completed a B.A. at the University of Waterloo (1996), and an M.A. at the University of Manitoba (1998). She is Poetry Co-Editor of Prairie Fire Magazine, and is currently completing her next book. Melanie was born in Kitchener-Waterloo in 1971 and now lives in Winnipeg.

JASON CAMLOT is the author of one collection of poems, *The Animal Library* (DC Books, 2000), recently nominated for the Quebec Writer's Federation A.M. Klein Prize for Poetry. He is Assistant Professor of English at Concordia University.

COREY FROST is a Montreal writer and performer currently studying in New York City. "Five minutes with the Communist Manifesto" is from his book *Tonight You'll Have a Filthy Dream*. His performances can be heard on CD ("Bits World: Exciting Version"), on radio, and occasionally on stage in Montreal, Toronto, or Vancouver.

KATE HALL is the co-editor of Delirium Press. She lives in Montreal. "Window I" and "Window II" are from a long poem entitled "Glass is a Slow Moving Liquid."

ADRIENNE HO's poetry chapbook *Murmur* was published by Junction Books in 2001. She lives, some of the time, in Montreal.

CATHERINE HUNTER's publications include the poetry collection *Latent Heat* (Signature Editions), the mystery thriller *The Dead of Midnight* (Turnstone Press) and the selected poetry audio CD, *Rush Hour* (Cyclops Press). She teaches English and Creative Writing at the University of Winnipeg.

JACK ILLINGWORTH was born and raised in Crooks Township, Ontario, and has shuffled between there, Montreal, and Toronto since attaining the age of majority seven years ago. He is the author of three still-growing manuscripts: *Panography*, *The Papers of Noah Job JAMUUNDSEN*, co-authored by Albuquerque whiz-kid Melissa Weinstein, and an as-yet untitled mongrel work about humiliating moments in nineteenth century science.

GEOFF LANSDELL is a Montreal writer and editor.

MONIQUE MACCLEOD is a Montreal writer.

DAPHNE MARLATT's latest collection of poems is *This Tremor Love Is* (Talonbooks).

CHANDRA MAYOR is a poet and editor. She has worked for dark leisure, Contemporary Verse 2, and Prairie Fire. Her first collection of poems, *August Witch* (Cyclops Press), will be released in the fall of 2002.

DAVID MCGIMPSEY was born and raised in Montreal. He is the author of several collections of poetry, the most recent being *Hamburger Valley, California* (ECW Press). He is also the author of the critical study *Imagining Baseball: America's Pastime and Popular Culture* (Indiana University Press) which was recently awarded the Popular Culture Association's award for Best Scholarly Study of the year.

KILBY SMITH-MCGREGOR is based in Toronto where she spends most of her time in the theatre. She is currently working on an adaptation of John Webster's *The Duchess of Malfi*, entitled *Cover Her Face*, with her company Stranger Theatre.

ROB MCLENNAN has published poetry, fiction and critical writing in Canada, USA, India, Australia, UK, and the Czech Republic. His most recent collection of poetry is *Paper Hotel* (Broken Jaw Press). The editor of four anthologies, including *You & Your Bright Ideas: New Montreal Writing* with Andy Brown (Véhicule) and *side/lines: A Poetics* (Insomniac), he lives in Ottawa.

Poet and playwright, **DANIEL DAVID MOSES** is a Delaware, born at Ohsweken on the Six Nations lands along the Grand River in southern Ontario, Canada. He lives in Toronto where he writes full time and is an associate artist with Native Earth Performing Arts. His most recent publications are *Sixteen Jesuses*, poems, *Brebeuf's Ghost*, a play, (both Exile Editions) and new editions of the plays *Almighty Voice and His Wife* (Playwrights Canada Press) and *Coyote City*, included with *City of Shadows* in Necropolitei: two plays (Imago).

HAL NIEDZVIECKI is editor of Broken Pencil, the magazine of zine culture and the independent arts (www.brokenpencil.com). His work of cultural criticism, *We Want Some Too: Underground Desire and the Reinvention of Mass Culture* was published by Penguin Canada in Spring 2000. In Fall 2001, Random House Canada published Hal's novel *Ditch*, a coming of age cyber-porn thriller. Said the Globe and Mail: "Challenging, bravely original and skillfully executed....but also creepy, sickening, and possibly downright offensive...This is one of the riskiest undertakings by a Canadian writer of Niedzviecki's generation, and it undoubtedly succeeds."

JOHN K. SAMSON drinks and sleeps in Winnipeg. He is the co-founder of Arbeiter Ring Publishing and lyricist for The Weakerthans. He recently starred in "Spring Chickens," a short baseball film directed by Matt Holm.

STEVE SMITH is a Toronto writer.

CARMINE STARNINO is a Montreal poet and critic. His most recent book of poems is *Credo* (McGill Queens Press).

SARAH STEINBERG is a Toronto writer and editor living in Montreal.

MICHELLE STERLING lives triumphantly.

KATE STERNS was born in Toronto in 1961 and grew up in Kingston Ontario. Her latest novel is *Down There by the Train* (Knopf Canada).

JULIA TAUSCH is a graduate student in Creative Writing and English Literature at Concordia University.

Originally from the Ottawa Valley, **MELISSA A. THOMPSON** is a Montreal artist and writer. She currently pursuing research in the areas of Women's Auto(bio)graphical Practices at Goldsmiths College University of London, for which she has been awarded a research grant in the visual arts from Les Fonds FCAR. A contributing editor of Matrix magazine, a great deal of her written work has been published in the form of hand-crafted books and objects.

Editor

JON PAUL FIORENTINO is a Winnipeg writer and editor living in Montreal and Winnipeg. He is a contributing editor for Matrix Magazine. His collections of poetry include *hover* (Staccato/Turnstone), *transcona fragments* (Cyclops Press), and *resume drowning* (Broken Jaw Press). In August, 2002, he became editor of Cyclops Press.

Publication Notes

Adrienne Ho. *Murmur*. Toronto: Junction Books, 2001.

Michelle Sterling. "ohtokyo" first published in Headlight Anthology.

Daniel David Moses. "Buzz" and "How to make a Fish Sweat"
   first published in Prairie Fire.

Daphne Marlatt. *This Tremor Love Is*. Vancouver: Talonbooks, 2001.
 "booking passage" —quotes from Mary Barnard, *Sappho: A New
   Translation*. U.C. Press, 1958.
"in the current" —quotes from Helene Cixous and Mireille Call-Gruber,
   trans. Eric Prenowitz, *Rootprints*. Routledge, 1997.

Carmine Starnino. *Credo*. Montreal: McGill-Queens University Press,
   2000.

Kate Sterns. *Down There by the Train*. Toronto: Knopf Canada, 2000.

[TCR+] 02

[TCR+] 02, the expanded, multimedia, on-line edition of The Cyclops Review, edited by Jon Paul Fiorentino and Clive Holden, can be found at

[www.cyclopspress.com]

[TCR+] 02 will feature the following:

William Coady Maher, audio poet (Heidelberg/San Francisco)

A variety of recordings from the Tic.Toc International Festival of New Performance (Victoria+)

Excerpts from the *Encyclopedia of Underwater Investigations*, by Rob Kovitz, book artist (Winnipeg)

War As Crime, an audioscape drama by Jurgen Hesse (Vancouver)

Excerpts from the novel *The Beautiful Dead End*, by Clint Hutzulak, and samples from the full-length soundtrack album to accompany the book (Victoria)

A selection of international audio/media art performances from Send + Receive, a Festival of Sound (Winnipeg+)

links to The Cyclops Review 02 contributors' personal & related sites.

AVAILABLE FROM CYCLOPS PRESS

For more information, visit www.cyclopspress.com. All titles are available in Canada thru Signature Editions, except where noted; international customers, please see our website.

Virgo Out Loud, Seán Virgo,
  ISBN 1-894177-07-X, 16.95, Audio CD (Fiction)

Blindsight, Ricardo Sternberg,
  ISBN 1-894177-03-7, 16.95, Audio CD (Poetry)

Necropsy of Love, Al Purdy,
  ISBN 1-894177-01-0, 16.95, Audio CD (Poetry)

August Witch, Chandra Mayor,
  ISBN 1-894177-12-6, 13.95, Book (Poetry)

Patrick Lane in Cab 43, Patrick Lane,
  ISBN 1-894177-04-5, 16.95, Audio CD (Poetry)

In The First Early Days of My Death, Catherine Hunter,
  ISBN 1-894177-14-2, 13.95, Book (Fiction)

Rush Hour, Catherine Hunter,
  ISBN 1-894177-08-8, 16.95, Audio CD (Poetry)

trains of winnipeg, Clive Holden,
    ISBN 1-894177-10-X, 16.95, Audio CD (Poetry)
    (thru Signature Editions or Endearing Records)

Fury: Fictions & Films, Clive Holden,
    ISBN 1-894177-00-2, 11.95, Book (Fiction)
    (from Arbeiter Ring Publishing in Canada)

transcona fragments, Jon Paul Fiorentino,
    ISBN 1-894177-11-8, 14.95, Book (Poetry)

The Cyclops Review, Jon Paul Fiorentino, Ed.,
    ISBN 1-894177-13-4, 13.95 Book (Anthology)

Local Scores, Terrance Cox,
    ISBN 1-894177-09-6, 16.95 Audio CD (Poetry)